Grand

Designs

Dedicated to all the people in the series who have
been brave enough to build their own homes

Grand
Designs

Building your Dream Home

Kevin McCloud
with Fanny Blake

CHANNEL 4 BOOKS

First published in 1999 by Channel 4 Books,
an imprint of Macmillan Publishers Ltd,
25 Eccleston Place, London SW1W 9NF and Basingstoke.

Associated companies throughout the world.

ISBN 0 7522 1355 5

10 9 8 7 6 5 4 3 2 1

A CIP catalogue record for this book is available from the British
Library.

Design by Bradbury and Williams
Special photography by Graeme Strong
Additional photography by Edward Schneider
(Detailed picture credits can be found on page 192.)
Colour reproduction by Speedscan Ltd
Printed by Bathpress Colourbooks, Glasgow

TalkBack

This book accompanies the television series *Grand Designs* made
by TalkBack Features for Channel 4.
Devised and Edited by Daisy Goodwin
Executive Producer: Peter Fincham
Series Producer: John Silver

Notes

The author, the publishers, their assigns, licensees and printers
cannot accept liability for any errors or omissions contained
herein nor liability for any loss to any person acting as a result of
the information contained in this book. This book gives advice on
the basis that readers contemplating designing and building their
own homes take their own professional advice.

All plans and drawings are for information only, not for
construction.

Contents

Introduction

For most of us the idea of building our own home represents an impractical dream. There are a thousand reasons why we may never get around to it, and why we may never want to. Popular excuses include: 'the children are growing up – they're at that crucial stage when exams mean everything', 'we haven't got the money', 'work's too demanding', 'I'm not practical' or even 'we're too old'. However, all these protestations can fall away, like scales from the eyes, when an ordinary homeowner like you or me gets the self-build bug.

Filming the series *Grand Designs*, we have seen suit-wearing fathers of 2.4 children become overnight disciples of solar power, power-dressing mothers leave their chargecards on the hall table and step out into a brave new world of composting toilets, and retired couples experience Damascene conversions to ecological living. From all this, it would seem that any one of us can unsuspectingly fall prey to a cult which is growing in numbers, not just in Britain but also around the world. There is a contained explosion happening in the building industry, of ordinary people who feel that it is about time that houses were designed and built for the individuals who occupy them, and built with a sense of how we live today.

This is understandable, given the way that the majority of new housing is thrown up in this

Below: Time spent carefully thinking about the site brings its own rewards.

country. The average development may consist of executive detached homes, squeezed onto little territorial plots and arranged in an exclusive (and excluding) cul-de-sac. Or it might be row after row of sham period semis, each terrace differing in some inconsequential detail, such as the colour of the chimney stack. Georgian was a popular 1980s style for this particular model. It has since been supplanted by Victorian and pastiche Edwardian prototypes. Whatever the design, these estates offer little in the way of excellence in craftsmanship and good ergonomic design. They are drawn up by draughtsmen from copybook patterns and constructed for profit. Rooms are small with low ceilings, plumbing and electrics are arranged for ease of installation, and insulation and other eco- (and wallet-)friendly elements are skimped. For example, our national minimum requirement for insulation in buildings is among the lowest in Europe.

Top and above: Unimaginative British housing developments are often thrown up without a thought for the surrounding environment, resulting in rows of identical boxes springing up all over Britain.

As to ergonomics, the way in which houses are arranged today has a great deal to do with the formalization of family life back in the early eighteenth century when the kitchen was at the back of the house and the dining/living rooms to one side, off a hall. Yet when you consider how we live now, how much time we spend at home, how much of that is spent in the kitchen, and how we like to juggle cooking with entertainment, it makes so much sense to devote the largest area in the house to a kitchen-cum-dining room, with a sofa in the corner and a television to one side.

It's the arrangement that many families adopt in farmhouse kitchens as the kitchen is easily the largest room in the home and it's an idea that should be emulated across the land. It means that you can prepare food while you talk to your guests or mind the children, cook, eat and relax in the same space, or get the shopping into the house without carrying it all the way to the back, and even keep an eye on what's going on in the street. As a design idea, it is not exactly the core

Above: Victorian terraces make up a large part of British housing stock, but do they suit the way we live now?

element of a radical approach to housing, but it is a simple example that shows how fundamentally modern housing does not suit our needs.

The Self-builders

Dissatisfaction with so much of Britain's current housing stock has led many people to consider designing and building their own home. In this book, we follow the fortunes of eight, very different sets of self-builders and their projects.

• Denys and Marjorie Randolph, a retired couple in their seventies, opted for a barn-style house in Oxfordshire for their second self-build project. This was designed for them by architect Roderick James.

• Rob Roy and Alida Saunders went completely green and built an eco-house complete with composting toilets in Suffolk. It was designed for them by Neil Winder.

• Birmingham-based Jane Fitzsimons and Gavin Allen bought a disused Methodist chapel in Gavin's native Cornwall, and local architect David Sheppard designed a conversion for them that would suit their home and work lifestyles as Gavin travels a lot in his job and Jane works for a computer company that encourages working from home.

• Tim Cox and Julia Brock opted for a quick-build kit house on their stunning Sussex coast location for their new baby and four daughters.

• Michael Hird and Lindsay Harwood went modernist-minimalist with a controversial concrete and glass structure in suburban Doncaster. It was designed by Lindsay's architect brother, Colin Harwood.

• Architect couple Sarah Wigglesworth and Jeremy Till's project was deliberately innovative as they wanted to build a house with walls made of straw bales, sand bags and gabion cages (a feature of motorway construction) by an inner-city railway line in Islington, London.

• Andrew Tate was also an architect with a dream. Andrew, with his partner Deborah Mills helping to manage the project, took on planners to convert an old water tower and to build on a modern extension in a Green Belt area.

• Ten young, and mostly unemployed, families built their own houses in Brighton by exchanging thirty hours of labour a week for cheap rent, in a ground-breaking deal with a housing association.

As we filmed and interviewed these people, it became pretty clear that they shared one thing in common: a sense of commitment and a belief that what they were doing was really the start of a new part of their lives. In some cases we even got the impression that they had undergone some kind of religious conversion. What they were building was not only a new house, but also a whole new world for themselves.

Given the attachment that we have to our dwellings, this belief is not at all surprising. Most of us who are homeowners are aware of an irrational and slightly inflated sense of territorialism that we ascribe to our property and its boundaries.

Below: Large open spaces – such as this one – with room to cook, eat, play and relax, are the kind of rooms that many people aspire to today. Very often the only way to achieve this is to build it yourself.

Overleaf: Hedgehog Housing Co-op members are building their own houses – with their own hands.

The anthropological view of this behaviour is that we see our land in purely tribal terms and are desperate to fend off any violation of it. Our homes are our castles – they are our caves and our territory – and we mark our territory out with chain-link fences, aggressive-looking dogs and signs that say 'No Turning, Private Drive'. I cannot point the finger here, since I am as guilty, and as primitive, as the next man or woman.

However, this overdeveloped sense of ownership of space can be a good thing. It is what drives some of us to better the places in which we live and to respect them. Many of the self-builders in this book feel that the homes they have built are not only better homes for themselves, but they also represent possible models for general housebuilding in the future. And perhaps some of them, like the Hedgehog Housing Co-op's buildings and Rob Roy's eco-home, are good examples of this. These are designs that would have been dismissed as cranky twenty years ago. Now, thanks to technology and perhaps a changing cultural view of how architecture should serve us and our lives, such schemes are on the verge of becoming mainstream.

'Common Ground'

What is interesting is that nearly all of the projects share several key features that point to the next few decades. Firstly, they all adopt an open-plan approach to downstairs living, combining kitchen and living areas. Denys and Marjorie's oak-framed home is designed as an atrium with satellite rooms in two wings. Andrew's design for his family's living area comprises one large space measuring 11 metres (36 feet) across with glass walls at either end. The

idea is that temporary screens will divide the space according to how it is needed at any one time, changing throughout the years.

Secondly, all our builders see the landscape environment of the building as not only related to, but also part of, a building's design. There is a current fashion to

Above: The chapel at Chilsworthy that Jane and Gavin bought for conversion.

extend the living space out into the garden with terraces, structures and verandahs, and many of our protagonists succumbed to the appeal of these devices. But for many of them, this approach goes far deeper: they are designing their outdoor spaces not just as external rooms, but also as gardens and courtyards which reflect the same ethos that determines the building. Andrew's scheme is an enclosed terrace occupying the space outside one glass wall, which is sheltered by the same earth bank as the house, and Rob and Alida's garden is laid out according to the same bio-dynamic principles as their eco-home. Meanwhile, the Hedgehog Housing Co-op share some outdoor spaces, as well as their build, and Jane and Gavin have incorporated a sunken indoor 'heavenly' garden into the design of their chapel conversion. If these projects illustrate anything, it is that garden and landscape design in Britain is undergoing a renaissance, driven not by the whims of designers but by the excitement of new homeowners and their philosophies. Our examples also go to show that when anyone embarks on building a dream house, what can often follow is a radical approach to the garden as well.

The third key feature of nearly all of the builds is the extraordinary way in which environmentally friendly issues have been taken on board. Only one of the projects is a self-declared eco-house, but many of the principles that its owners, Rob and Alida, espouse have also been taken up by several of the other self-builders as a matter of course. The Hedgehog Housing Co-op were building wooden houses according to a self-build pattern laid down by the architect Walter Segal in the 1960s. Segal's methodology did not initially champion environmentalism, it wasn't a popular issue then, but the building style happens to be naturally green and has since adapted itself to embrace every element of sustainability.

Perhaps the most unlikely converts to ecology were Denys and Marjorie, who are both pensioners. Denys is the retired chairman of Wilkinson Sword. Their oak barn build incorporates a plethora of green values, many of them subtle, such as the sustainability of the native-managed hardwood used for the frame, and the fact that the forest from which it came, and the yard in which it was constructed, are within 100 miles of the site. This means low transport costs and minimal 'embodied energy' (see page 146).

Denys and Marjorie left a previous self-build and a large established vineyard to come to this house. Their conversion to contemporary design and the values of a 'green' life has been both rational and gradual, but none the less impressive. The couple's new home quietly boasts high-technology thermal glazing, underfloor heating supplied from a heat pump (trapping passive solar energy), and an

Opposite: It only took one glimpse of the Coleshill water tower looming through the mist for Andrew to know that he and his family had to live there whatever obstacles might lie in their path.

arrangement of rooms and windows designed to maximize direct heating from the sun. Outside, they are making their peace with the world by cultivating a flower meadow and wildlife pond.

The Five Self-build Commandments

So having completed their dream home, what did our self-builders have to say about it all? What guiding principles can they hand down to us, if we're thinking of embarking upon that same journey?

• Without doubt, every self-builder underestimates the amount of planning needed. Whether you are simply overseeing progress or sawing every plank and pipe yourself, it is clear that good logistics, good records and good management are important elements. The build wants to take over your life. Planning and management help you fight back, and this book is a versatile tool that can help you to do that.

• Flexibility was a word that kept cropping up whenever I interviewed anyone, be it a builder, homeowner or architect. Compromise may be the enemy of good design and rigid obstinacy may see a project through, but the best buildings in the world are the ones which result from their owners and architects listening and co-operating with each other. Cross-fertilization of ideas and the exchange of inspiration are the means by which great and original schemes are born. So fight your corner, but learn from others involved in the build.

• Many of our self-builders overestimated their own abilities to think the project into reality and so discovered that they had no 'spatial mind'. We all feel that we are expected to understand technical drawings and elevations, especially if we have pretensions of being builders ourselves, but the truth

Opposite: Tim and Julia's 'glorified beach hut' is finished at last.

of the matter is that even architects and designers need help in envisioning how a building might look. Models and coloured drawings are an essential and much undervalued tool here. A full architect's model can help you to understand the space and volumes of your home, but insist also that your model is coloured and not left in that minimal balsa finish (so clean, but not so convenient for addressing all those unresolved areas of finish and detail). At the very least, you could make your own model by sticking your elevation drawings onto card, colouring them in and then glueing them together. In addition to this, research all your building materials, get samples of them and put them together to see how they blend. The result is always worth while and an education in itself.

• Nearly everyone I spoke to emphasized the need to work alongside professionals, especially when you are building for the first time. Whether it is at the design, planning or building stage, any project will benefit hugely from the care of a professional adviser. It is foolish to think that you can manage without help, especially from an architect, and ultimately you can probably save money by consulting others. Other services are provided by project managers, quantity surveyors, soil engineers, planning agents, structural engineers and building surveyors. But don't be put off by this list: this book will help you to decide who you need to work with, and also when.

• Finally, there is no doubt that the abiding qualities you need as a self-builder are a sense of vision and commitment. The ex-traveller members of the Hedgehog Housing Co-op allowed themselves over two years in which to build their houses, during which time they expected to have no social life and very little private life. For even the most relaxed and organized of our builders (and this includes the architects supervising the building of their own homes) the stakes were high and disaster could strike at any point, whether during planning, financing or building. Hope, belief and dogged determination may all be required in order to achieve your dream.

But, and it is a big but, there is something wonderful that comes from commitment and determination, something that filled our builders with an almost apostolic zeal and a twinkle in the eye: it is the great sense of adventure that building a house brings. There are not many experiences in life which we can claim as truly epic. Maybe the birth of a child comes close for some, while sailing round the world for a year, crossing the Sahara, trekking to the North Pole, or climbing Everest may figure on other people's lists. Perhaps you have a novel inside you that is itching to be written. Each of us has a tailored ambition, our own personal goal to one day achieve, and for many people that goal is to build a house.

And it's easy to see why. Our ancestors built defences around their caves, constructed castles and bastides, and raised edifices to mark every aspect of human life. The need to build is a very primitive one. It is partly a need to make secure, partly a wish to provide for one's kin and partly an aim to make some kind of permanent mark. As a process, building something solid and tangible is, for most of us, an unusual and life-enriching experience where a team of people learn to work together. Building your own home, to your own designs, can be a dream come true and it can, at the same time, be fraught with excitement and horrors, a drama where even swashbuckling antics and eleventh-hour rescue missions occur. It is one of the last great adventures open to us.

Below: Denys and Marjorie's dream home is built – but it takes time for that building site look to go.

Finding
a Site

1

Before you can seriously get to grips with the idea of building your dream home, you need the land on which to do it. A favourite estate agents' maxim is 'Location, location, location . . .' for the very reason that it is the one thing that has an enormous bearing on every aspect of your home. Just how easy is it to find an appropriate plot? Have no illusions about this: it isn't at all simple. Like anything else, when you want something urgently you can never find it and when you're least expecting to find it, it just turns up. Finding a plot is certainly considered to be one of the worst hurdles that self-builders have to overcome. Don't imagine that you're going to walk out and find the ideal spot immediately. Be prepared to wait until the right property turns up and don't compromise until you absolutely have to. Compromise in the early stages is the great enemy of good design. Only you can define the area in which you want to live, by taking into account its proximity to, or distance from, the things that may be important to you, such as shops, schools and your work. You also need to know the proposed size of house you will be building so you can look for an appropriately sized plot. However, keep the ideas for the style in which you want to build reasonably flexible at this stage, since the plot itself and local planners may dictate that you go down a road that you would never have otherwise considered.

Where to Look

The most obvious way to embark on your search for land is by trying local estate agents. Don't leave this to just a single visit or phone call: keep on badgering them, making sure they know you're serious by being as precise as you can in the detail of what you are looking for. You need to persuade them to contact you, rather than the local builder or developer, should a site come up that they think might be suitable for your self-build.

The one thing Rob Roy and Alida Saunders were quite clear about was that they wanted to remain in Suffolk, close to their friends, community and family. Because of their concerns about global warming, they wanted to live in a place that was protected, where there would be no danger from potential rises in the sea level over the next forty or fifty years. The setting was to be rural, with enough land to have a productive garden, while the house needed a south-facing aspect to gain maximum benefit from solar energy. They concentrated their search principally through estate agents and it took only five or six weeks before they hit gold: 'The plot had planning permission for a lavish mansion and had been on the market for five or six years, but the price had eventually halved and we fell in love with it, despite its being covered with brambles and weeds.'

You can also read the property advertisements in local and national papers, not forgetting *Exchange & Mart* and *Daltons Weekly*. Denys and Marjorie Randolph

Below: If your heart is set on building in the Green Belt or in an Area of Outstanding Natural Beauty, the only way forward may be 'bungalow gobbling', building on the site of an existing building. This is what Denys and Marjorie decided they had to do when they first saw this stunning view of the Chilterns.

saw their plot advertised in the *Oxford Times*: 'It was an advertisement for a bungalow with two photographs, one of the building and one of the view. The bungalow was very dilapidated, which was fine because we knew we wanted to rebuild. When we walked through the gate and looked at the view right across the Chiltern Hills we knew this had to be it. We put in an offer.'

Railway contractor Michael Hird and his wife Lindsay Harwood noticed their Doncaster plot, which was advertised in the property section of a local free sheet, quite by chance. The council was selling off the site of a mock-Tudor building used to house the grass-cutters for the local playing fields. Andrew Tate and Deborah Mills were idly leafing through the Sunday papers on a French beach when they found their plot. So it does pay to keep your eyes open.

The self-build magazines carry advertisements for land-finding agencies with whom you can register for a fee. Although you may find their lists are unavoidably out of date, they can point you in the right direction. Many of them have extensive displays at the national self-build shows and it may be worth your while to pay them a visit. (Although the shows are very useful, you'll find the emphasis is on practicalities of building rather than design and new ideas. This is not the place for real inspiration.)

Why not advertise for land in the local press yourself, or put an ad in the local builders' merchants? Use your initiative and offer some sort of incentive (a financial one will probably reap the best rewards) for the person who finds you the right plot. Write to local builders or farmers. It is possible that a developer may be prepared to sell off an unwanted site. Architects, surveyors and solicitors are also worth a try. Other bodies, such as the water or electricity companies, the Church or the railway companies, may own land in your chosen area which could include an ideal site for individual development. Find out the best person to approach and write to them. If you don't already know people living in the area, put out the word in the pub or local shops. At all times be as specific as you can about exactly what it is that you are looking for.

Below: Paul Crouch, one of the founders of the Hedgehog Housing Co-op.

If you've decided that instead of designing and building a home of your own from scratch, you would prefer to buy a kit home from one of the packaging companies operating in this country (many of them advertise in the self-build magazines), they too may be able to help you in your search. After all, it's in their interests to assist a prospective client in finding somewhere they can build.

Search for Yourself

If all the above suggestions draw a blank, there are ways to identify a site on your own. Go to the local planning office and take a look through the planning applications file. It may be that you'll find a prospective vendor has applied for outline planning permission (see Chapter 5, Get Planning, pages 92–109) before putting the property on the market. Check the Local Plan, which shows exactly what planning policies exist for the area and you may identify a site designated for development that hasn't been touched yet. Both these sources of information are open to the public and if – like Paul Crouch of the Hedgehog Housing Co-op – you are turned away you can still insist on your rights. Paul was

a traveller who, with his partner, had decided to curtail their life on the road and form a housing co-operative to build their own homes. He had spotted the site from his caravan on the other side of the valley and wanted to investigate its availability. Because the authorities assumed he wanted to use it as somewhere to park his caravan, Paul was refused access to the Plan. He stood his ground and was eventually able to see that the plot was one of two that had been set aside for social housing in Brighton. And so the Hedgehog Housing Co-op found its home.

Everything has its price so it's worth examining the local Ordnance Survey map closely. It may be possible to identify opportunities where a plot could be created, such as from two side gardens, a sizeable back garden or an orchard or paddock. All these are potential sites. Nothing ventured, nothing gained: if you contact them, the owners can only say no, but they might surprise you by agreeing to sell.

The most satisfactory way of locating your plot is to discover it for yourself. Use your imagination when it comes to envisaging the potential of an overgrown field or a rundown building. 'Bungalow gobbling' is a real option that is open to you; if a building already exists, it is quite possible that permission will be given to replace it with something else occupying the exact same spot or 'footprint'. Alternatively, you may be able to adapt and enlarge it, literally swallowing it up in a new architectural skin. District councils operate different policies in this regard, but it's always worth contacting them to check individual guidelines. If, like Denys and Marjorie, you are fortunate enough to find a rundown building for sale in an Area of Outstanding Natural Beauty, then the local council may sometimes be persuaded that rebuilding will improve the site. Otherwise it can be extremely difficult to initiate a new build in such an area.

Tim Cox and Julia Brock might never have built their own home at all if they hadn't been walking in an area of Newhaven, slightly off the beaten track, when they came across an overgrown gateway. Their curiosity aroused, Tim forced his way down the drive, through a garden that was nose-high with brambles and nettles, to a derelict 1930s breeze-block house. There he was bowled over by the unexpected and most spectacular cliff-top view of the sea. Most people would have left it there, but not Tim. Through talking with a local estate agent he discovered that not only was the land for sale but planning permission had been granted for a modern four-bedroomed house on the site.

Tim and Julia were convinced that it would be the perfect place for their young family to grow up. They also love sailing so the position of the plot was irresistible. Until they found the site, they hadn't seriously thought about self-building, but the opportunity to live in such a wonderful location was too good to pass up.

Should you have difficulty in finding out who owns a site, check with HM Land Registry, which holds a register of land ownership. These days the exchange of property ownership has to be registered with them, but if ownership stretches back a long way then you may be unable to trace the owner. In that case, try the neighbours, local estate agents, and even the local council. If no one emerges as the rightful owner, you could always take the huge risk of assuming that they never will, but it's better to give up gracefully and to look for somewhere else.

Below: Tim and Julia only had to see the view to know that this was where they wanted to live.

The other route to creating your own home is conversion. There has been a huge vogue for barn conversions throughout the country, but there are other possibilities too. For Andrew and Deborah the idea of building couldn't have been further from their minds when they were on holiday in the south of France: 'We had some newspapers on the beach

Above and right: Barn conversions like the one above are always popular but you can be limited by the local planning regulations. Building your own barn-like structure like the Carpenter Oak house shown right can give you the same feeling of space in the spot of your choice.

and one of the Sunday supplements had an article on the Elspeth Beard water tower in Godalming. The end of the piece featured other water towers for sale and one of them was at Coleshill, about ten miles from where we lived. When we got home I drove over to have a look. My first impression was that it was a lovely building but too close to the main road. But when Andrew saw it, he just said, "No, we're living there." Things progressed from there – we didn't make any conscious decisions to build our own house. It was the tower that inspired us.'

Jane Fitzsimons, sales manager for a computer company, and management consultant Gavin Allen were similarly unprepared when they found the Methodist chapel that they have converted into a home: 'Gavin was born and bred in Cornwall, and we'd been looking for somewhere to live as a second home but couldn't find anything suitable – they just didn't give us the space we wanted. We were visiting Gavin's father in Cornwall and he mentioned the local Methodist chapel was up for auction. We looked around it and couldn't believe the space and the terrific views.'

If you're hunting for a site in a town or city, then you'll have your work cut out unless, like Michael and Lindsay, you spot it by chance. Property is extremely hard to find and is usually snapped up by developers without the agents giving the individual self-builder much of a look-in. London-based architects Jeremy Till and Sarah Wigglesworth started looking for a site about five years ago when they began getting sales catalogues and going to auctions. If you do manage to find somewhere it will most likely be a 'brown-field' site. This means it will already have a building on it and that you will have to demolish this and rebuild in its place.

What to Watch Out For

Once you have identified your prospective site, take a good hard look at it. It's up to you to spot any obvious conditions which may impact on the price of the build and on its positioning. It is important to watch out for sloping ground. In this case you may have to level the ground or radically alter your plans to accommodate the fall by building back into the slope or adding an unplanned basement level. Like Denys and Marjorie, you may be able to take advantage of the situation by sinking a hot tub into the extra underfloor depth at one end of the building. Of course, if you're adopting a more unorthodox approach (as in the case of the Hedgehog Housing Co-op, who built on stilts), then this will not cause a problem.

Secondly, look out for any trees on the site. Are they far enough away from where you want to build? If not, remember that planners often have a great

fondness for trees and hate to see them chopped down. In conservation areas there may be restrictions, in any case. If you do get permission to remove a tree, subsidence may become a problem as a result, and you may have to plant another elsewhere. Tim and Julia had a nasty moment when their foundations were being dug and they found tree roots were invading a trench, but fortunately they only had to lose one tree to solve the problem.

The third principle thing to watch out for is ground conditions. Walk around the property and see if there are any tell-tale signs of damp ground. Has the land been used as a dumping ground? Is it the site of an old pond? Take into account anything that may have a bearing on the foundations you're going to be sinking. If they need to go deep, your pockets will have to match.

Other practicalities that could be potentially problematic are the existence of overhead cables or underground drainage, both of which will need to be re-routed. It is essential too that you check your access to mains connections for electricity, gas and water. If there is access to the public sewer then make sure it is below the level of your site. The same goes for an existing septic tank, or you may find yourself, like Tim and Julia, having to invest an unbudgeted £3,000 or so in a mini treatment plant, which can discharge water into a nearby watercourse. If there isn't a nearby public sewer to which you can be connected, then you may alternatively, like Denys and Marjorie, have to invest in a septic tank (which will need to be emptied once a year) or a cess pit (which needs to be emptied anything from between six to twelve times a year). Alternatively you may want to instal a composting toilet as Sarah and Jeremy have done.

Talk to neighbours or even visit the local library to find out more about the history of the property. It's a good idea to visit the site at night and at different times of the day to make sure that you're not downwind of the local pig farm, a New Age festival site, or unexpectedly close to the late-night radioactive waste disposal train. Your solicitor can also visit the site for you, but they won't necessarily do this unless you ask them to. If you are in doubt about anything, always ask your solicitor.

Planning Restrictions and Legal Considerations

What access is there to the land? Will you be involved in the expense of building a long driveway with a turning point? Heavy vehicles are going to have to be able to reach the site and it should be accessible for transporting materials. Local highway authorities are very particular about visibility splays (areas free from

Opposite: Jane and Gavin had been searching for a new house for a while when Gavin's father told them the Methodist chapel at Chilsworthy was up for auction.

obstructions that could block the view of traffic entering, leaving or driving past the property). Check also that you haven't got a footpath running right through the spot you've earmarked for your sitting room. It's also worth confirming that the land boundaries defined by the vendor coincide with those in the deeds. We've all heard too many reports about the grief that comes from neighbours arguing over the position of a fence.

Your solicitor will deal with the title and local searches, plus any other legal ramifications. A ransom strip may exist between the site and the main road. This is a strip of land usually owned by someone other than the vendor as a safeguard against unwelcome development. It may be problematic or even impossible to buy it, so it's essential that you should be aware of its existence at an early stage in your considerations. There may be prohibitive covenants that are being passed down with the sale, as there were in the eighteen-page document supplied by British Rail to Sarah and Jeremy that, among other things, prevented them from building

Below: Deborah thought the tower was too close to the road but Andrew convinced her of its potential as a home for their young family.

within a certain distance of the railway line. You also need to check if there are any easements on the property (where other people have restricted use of your land for running drains or other services across it). These may be expensive to re-route.

If you're satisfied in all the above regards, then one very important consideration still remains. Does the land come with planning permission? It is deemed madness to buy a plot without at least outline permission (see Chapter 5, Get Planning, pages 92–109). There may be good reason why the land hasn't been singled out for development. You need to know why or you may end up with a horribly expensive and useless bit of grazing!

How to Buy

Once you are in a position to buy the land, the rest can be quite straightforward and your solicitor will then proceed to act on your behalf, very much in the same way as if you were buying a house, moving to exchange of contracts and then completion some weeks later. However, sometimes things are not so simple.

Having decided they wanted to buy the Coleshill water tower, Andrew and Deborah went to the estate agents named in the article they had spotted to begin proceedings. However, they were told that the property was not going on the market until the agents had received outline planning permission. Andrew then approached Three Valleys Waterboard directly by letter, offering them £50,000 and asking them to talk to him first before approaching the planners so that he could put forward his ideas for the tower's development: 'The next day there was a message on my answerphone from the water board, saying they were going to meet the planners the following day but would like to talk to me – total serendipity. They delayed the meeting, we met and they accepted our offer.'

Or did they? The person they'd been dealing with then went to Australia, and when Andrew and Deborah's offer went before the board it was agreed that in order to satisfy the shareholders that they were getting the full market value for the site, it should be placed on the open market. 'The first we knew was on a Saturday morning when the estate agents' details dropped through our letterbox! I kicked up as much fuss as I dared, but eventually they received three offers, of which ours was the lowest. However, apparently it was the most credible and we were told that if we matched the middle offer, it would be ours.'

But the story was far from over. Without planning permission, the idea was worth nothing so Andrew and Deborah paid £1 for an option on the land. This was to last for eighteen months, during which time they would fight to gain permission for the conversion and a new building. On gaining it, they would immediately pay the balance of the selling price. The price of an option is something you can agree with the vendor – it could be as little as £1 or as much as ten per cent of the purchase price. It's all down to your negotiating skills.

Alternatively, it's possible to buy at auction. It's always advisable to be very firm with yourself about how far you're prepared to go and to stop at that price. If you feel you may get carried away in the heat of the moment then ask someone else to go along and bid for you, though it seems a shame to miss the excitement. You may only have a very short time but you're well advised to prepare your finances and to do all the relevant checks first because once the gavel falls on your bid, there's no going back. You may not be quite as lucky as Jane and Gavin, who were so certain they wouldn't be successful at the auction, they didn't bother getting a formal survey done. Gavin knew the area and was sure there weren't any mining works beneath the building and got a builder friend to check it out. The guide price was £60,000 for the chapel, with the land at a fixed price of £15,000 on top of that.

Then came the day of the auction and Jane took the day off work while Gavin was away on business. 'There were four bidders at the start, but I knew I shouldn't bid immediately – I've seen how it's done on television! I ended up bidding against another couple, but I'd heard them talking to the auctioneers earlier, asking if they could take an option on the land to buy it later, so I guessed they must have quite a strict limit. I was enjoying it because I didn't think we were really going to get it. When, at £84,000, we did, everyone was staring at me. It wasn't till I got to the car that I shrieked and phoned Gavin.' Ten per cent of the purchase price must be paid to the auctioneers there and then, with the balance due a month later, but Jane and Gavin had not been well advised and this was to prove an unforeseen problem (see Chapter 6, Money Matters, pages 110–123).

Sarah and Jeremy were also fortunate in eventually buying a site at auction, but numerous difficulties immediately reared their heads, not least an unwanted tenant – a family business that forged springs for London taxis – who had absolutely no wish to leave. 'We only saw it a week before the auction and there was not much we could do in the way of checks. You do get more information up front than you do for a normal sale – you're given all the legal convenants and the local authority searches. We had a cursory visit to the site, made difficult by the fact that there were tenants. As it was being sold by Railtrack, it came with an eighteen-page covenant which, among such conditions as our not being able to plant trees on the site, did contain something about the relationship between the building and the

nearest electrical cable, which we didn't fully understand at the time. In fact, it was to do with how close to the track itself we could safely build. Our misunderstanding meant that we had to redesign the building!

'We phoned the planning department – which everyone should do as a matter of course – to check that redevelopment of the plot had been approved in principle. But mistakenly, we didn't go to the planners to see the Local Plan so we

Above: Jane and Gavin had to consult their new neighbours and think through the impact on the local scenery before they could do anything to the exterior of the chapel.

Above: Sarah and Jeremy were undeterred by their proximity to the railway line. However, misunderstanding part of the covenant that came with the plot meant they had to redesign their building so it sat further away than they had originally envisaged.

didn't know that it was on the boundary of a conservation area. So whatever we built might be considered to impact on that. We did a back-of-the-envelope desperately optimistic calculation and on the basis of that we set ourselves a limit for bidding. But our worst mistake was to do with the tenant. All the documents said the lease was up in six months' time but the family had been there for fifty years and didn't want to move. So, in the face of this refusal, we became liberal landlords and remained so for about the next two-and-a-half years!'

A less common way of buying property in England is by tender, or sealed bids, though it is the norm in Scotland. After seeing the Doncaster plot advertised, Michael called the local council to find out exactly where it was. Both he and Lindsay want their children, Max and Linden, to grow up streetwise so it had always been their plan to move from the country when they were approaching their teens. As it turned out, the site was ideal, being close to the centre of the town, on the edge of playing fields and a couple of minutes' walk from Lindsey's mother: Michael hadn't done any research into the land whatsoever and valued it by thinking of a figure he would be comfortable paying. 'We didn't think, what's the going rate for land? Because there's almost no land in towns, you're always up against developers. We were lucky and caught them on the hop.' Weeks later the council phoned and asked if the bid was still valid. If it was, the land was Michael's on payment of ten per cent immediately, with the rest due at the council's request. 'It was almost like an impulse buy. Don't you think when you do something off the cuff in life, it's always better than something you've carefully planned? We were very lucky.'

Becoming the owner of that ideal piece of land or that property ripe for conversion is just the beginning of an adventure that will bring its fair share of frustrations and rewards. But once you've got it, you're in a position to start making your plans become a reality.

Below: The old forge on the Islington site.

Do You Need an Architect?

2

Do you need an architect to help you to create your dream home? Andrew Tate, Jeremy Till and Sarah Wigglesworth are all architects, and have spent seven years gaining the relevant qualifications, knowledge and opinions. But what about the rest of us? Determined to have the home we've always wanted, won't an architect override our wishes, take the budget sky high and charge exorbitant fees on top? Not if you're careful and follow some fairly straightforward guidelines.

What They Can Contribute

Think of what an architect can contribute to your build. For a start, they have professional training that, far from being designed to counteract your ideas, is intended to make the most of them and to solve any problems that may arise in achieving them. They have technical skills that will be invaluable to you when it comes to drawing up the detailed plans, making models or creating persuasive documents for submission for planning permission and building regulations. Their experience with similar building projects will help you to avoid the usual pitfalls of a beginner.

Architects will also have contacts ranging from people in the planning department and building inspectors to the many different sub-contractors you'll be employing on your site, and they will know all the ropes. For example, they will be able to advise you on the most strategic way to approach the planners, the need for a structural surveyor and the order in which the build should proceed. You could try to do all these things yourself, but be sure you have the time, energy and money, should things go wrong.

If you're concerned about the additional cost, then you can agree in advance exactly how much you want an architect to do. For example, if you only want them to provide the drawings and to leave you to manage the project and deal with the separate sub-contractors, say so and negotiate an appropriate fee. It seems clear from the experiences of our house owners that employing professional help, and as much of it as you can afford, ultimately makes the build easier, less stressful and sometimes cheaper.

How to Find an Architect

Because the land can throw various unforeseen problems at you, most people opt to find it first and then appoint an architect. But not so Denys and Marjorie Randolph, who were spurred on in their plans to find a site by seeing something on television: 'I saw this programme in February which featured work by the architect, Roderick James. Later I said, "Darling, that's the future." We sent off to the BBC for details immediately but we didn't find the plot until May.'

If an architect isn't fortuitously delivered into your sitting room by the magic box, how do you find one that you can trust? Should you be as fortunate as Michael Hird and Lindsay Harwood, you may already have one in the family. Lindsay's brother, Colin, designed their current home – a chapel conversion, with which they were very happy – and was keen to create something for them from

Left: Colin Harwood gets the measure of the Doncaster site.

scratch: 'Colin's taste is quite similar to ours so we knew we were going to get something we really liked.' Having an architect in the family has its advantages: 'It's reasonably priced and you can both be quite honest and open, and say what you really think.' And its disadvantages? 'It's less of a business relationship so you probably tolerate more delay, and so on. You're less likely to be firm in that sense.'

But for the majority of people who are less fortunate, then the next best route is through personal recommendation. Rob Roy knew that although he wanted to control his eco-build from start to finish, he needed an architect who understood sustainable building and the Walter Segal method of construction (see Chapter 4, Material Facts, pages 72–91) and who was aligned towards ecological buildings. He approached the Walter Segal Self-Build Trust and was directed towards various architects, to whom he talked but whom, for one reason or another, he didn't feel were right for the job: 'Then a friend recommended Neil Winder, who had just built his own house nearby in Diss, *not* using the Segal method. We met him and were completely inspired.'

If, like Tim Cox and Julia Brock, you opt for a kit home then the packager, in their case Unique Homes, will provide their own architect with whom you can work, modifying one of their standard designs to suit your needs. 'We went to the Self-Build Exhibition and looked at the different ways of building houses. We chose Unique Homes through impulsiveness. Thier representative came to see us and we liked what he had to say.'

If you're still drawing a blank, try the RIBA (Royal Institute of British Architects). They have a list of all the architects who are registered with them and their client advisory service will put forward up to six in your area, depending on your specifications, or alternatively three or four who specialize in the type of building in which you're interested. You're best advised to talk to all of them before you make your choice. Similarly, the Association of Self-Build Architects has a national network and should be able to put you in contact with an architect in your district.

Once the Hedgehog Housing Co-op had established a working relationship with the South London Family Housing Association, it was time to find a sympathetic architect who would be interested in designing the best housing

Below: Architect Neil Winder lives in an eco-house which he designed and built himself.

within the constraints imposed by social building. Paul Crouch and his fellow Co-op members approached three separate firms of architects, who in turn presented three quite different solutions. But as far as they were concerned, Robin Hillier of Architype empathized the most with what they wanted to achieve and came up with an appropriate design for their needs.

If all else fails, there's always the *Yellow Pages*. While living in Birmingham, Jane Fitzsimons and Gavin Allen wanted to employ a local architect to convert their Cornish Methodist chapel. It can be much more problematic to find the right architect if you live a long way from the site. They had no alternative but to take a chance and to let their fingers do the walking: 'We had met some London architects who were interested because of the scale of the building but we decided that, because we weren't local, having a local architect would be key because we knew we wanted them to project-manage a lot of it for us. So we went through the Yellow Pages. We did phone the RIBA and ASBA, but they were totally useless in our case. In the end we saw about seven or eight [architects]. It took a lot of time but it was definitely worth it, even though we settled for David Sheppard who had been recommended by our building society surveyors.' There is a good deal to be said for using a local architect who will have the local contacts you need and a thorough knowledge of local architecture and design, and, of course, the vagaries of the local planners.

What to Look For

If you haven't set your heart on a particular architect then it's essential to make sure that you choose one who is properly accredited and that you like their work. In the first instance, follow Jane and Gavin's example and interview several people. Most architects are members of the RIBA and are therefore registered with ARB (Architect's Registration Board), which they can only be if they have achieved the appropriate qualifications. If your architect is not a member of the RIBA, you should confirm that they are none the less registered with ARB.

An architect is as good as the work they have done, so don't be satisfied just by looking through an attractive and impressive portfolio. Get out there and look at the buildings themselves. Roderick James, the architect behind Denys and Marjorie's oak-frame build and chairman of Carpenter Oak & Woodland Co. Ltd, always encourages potential clients to visit his Devon office: 'I've got a whole range of buildings here that I can take them round. I just watch them very carefully and see the sort of questions they ask, and the sort of things that might worry them.

Opposite: Look at an architect's previous work before you appoint him. This is an artist's retreat designed by David Sheppard well before he embarked on the Chilsworthy chapel conversion.

We'll go through the whole process with lots of photographs, lots of drawings, different plans and ideas, and I'll get a feeling for what they want. There's no charge for that visit and people do find it incredibly useful.'

Rob and Alida visited Neil Winder at the home he had designed and built for himself: 'We had taken on board a lot of the energy-conscious building techniques, things like timber structures, having a corridor to the north of the property with spaces that don't need to be heated, such as the pantry or drying room, having a highly insulated structure, maximum window space on the south side, a verandah with a roof to maximize usable space, and so on. Neil's house is virtually the same so it really was an inspiration. He was very struck by how similar our design was to his house.'

If you can, talk to the clients that the architect has most recently worked with and satisfy yourself that their methods of working sound like the sort of thing you can live with. It's vital that you like your architect, that you feel a rapport with them over the work you will be asking them to carry out. It's no use admiring the work but loathing the person – it will almost certainly lead to disaster. Denys and Marjorie had recently been in Devon and seen some of Roderick James's work so they invited him to visit them in Oxfordshire: 'We immediately liked him and got on like a house on fire, which is absolutely essential. But he was rather concerned because he thought we wouldn't be happy living in a barn. The house we were living in was too well insulated, the doors fitted and everything was neat and tidy, and thought out. We pointed out that the one we'd lived in before that had been 300 years old, so we knew we would learn to live with a barn.'

The architect–client relationship is crucial to the success of your project. David Sheppard sums it up when he says: 'With any client you get to know about almost everything they do and that's why it's a very privileged position to be an architect, really. You have this rapport with them that is very confidential. You get to know them, to understand what their tastes are, what their feelings are, and what they expect of you.'

Costs

Finally, you should ask the architect you are considering about what and how they would charge you. Guidelines for this are set out by the RIBA, although they are not necessarily adhered to. There is a standard form of appointment that the architect can provide and you should make sure that it precisely defines the architectural services that will be provided, and identifies costs, fees and procedures. As for payment itself, it can be made in a number of ways, one of which you will agree suits you most.

- As a percentage of the total cost of the build. This is usually best on more straightforward projects, when the final cost can be pretty accurately estimated. Do clarify what is included in this and what is not.
- As a lump sum.
- On an hourly rate. This could range from £30 to £170 depending on the nature of the work, how specialized it is, and of course, the seniority of the architect within their practice. Architects tend to prefer this method of payment since it allows for unforeseen problems and the attendant work needed to solve them.

Normally, architects expect to be paid on a monthly basis, which will help you with your budget. However, you can also agree to pay in stages of work completed, e.g. outline proposals, scheme design, detail design, production information and work on site. Remember to hold a bit back in reserve so that they will come back at the end of the job to go over it and to check that there isn't any unfinished business.

As the work on site progresses, your architect will provide certificates at agreed intervals (usually four-weekly). These represent the stage payments due to the builder and are agreed with the architect before issue. The builder will have presented a detailed valuation of the work they've done for the architect to check. If it's incomplete or substandard, then the architect will alter the valuation accordingly. Otherwise the architect signs off the work and allows the builder to invoice.

Finally, do make sure that your architect has professional indemnity insurance so that in the event of something going wrong with the building, they are insured for a claim made against them.

The Role of the Client

Before an architect does any work for you, you will need to discuss the type of house you are after, giving them as detailed a brief as possible, conveying not only your ideas and preferences, but your dislikes too. Time spent in preliminary discussions is invaluable and can be key to the success or failure of your plans.

If, like Marjorie, you have a background in art, then you may be able to convey your ideas through drawing your own detailed sketches. Having decided that they definitely wanted to use Carpenter Oak, Denys and Marjorie spent days pouring

Right and below: Tim and Julia's original sketch, shown right, proves that you don't have to be a great draughtsman to get the result you want, as can be seen below.

over plans and trying to work out what they wanted: 'We almost lived in our conservatory in the old house so we knew we wanted another that faced south or south-east in the new place. We kept drawing L-shaped designs, trying to put a conservatory in the base of the L – and you can't do it. We gave Roderick the sort of layout we wanted – a carport, a lounge, conservatory and bedroom, and we always have a bathroom each. We sent him beautiful drawings of the bedroom and bathroom area, the living area, and the entrance hall and conservatory. I said: "This is marvellous. We've got two barns joined together by a conservatory and I haven't the faintest notion how you're going to construct that." He roared with laughter. The thing about Roderick is that he has brilliant flashes of ideas. He took one look at our drawings and said: "You want an atrium in the middle with a couple of wedges on either side." I knew immediately he was absolutely right.'

Tim and Julia spent a long evening over a bottle of wine while Julia sketched out their ideas: 'Initially, we had the idea of a building in a pyramid shape with glass at the apex, but then fantasy gave way to reality. We'd always fancied living in a giant beach hut. If I could have bought a ladder and joined the sea up, that's what I would have done. I planned the house based on what we needed, the way I thought we lived, and by standing for hours in our cottage with a tape measure, trying to imagine what 20 square feet looked like… and would it be enough space for us?'

If you're less confident in your drawing skills, it's an idea to build up some sort of scrapbook to include photos you've taken and magazine pictures of buildings or details you love. It is just as important to be as clear about what you don't want as what you do want, but be flexible enough to be responsive to your architect's ideas. Jane and Gavin were quite definite: 'We did have some ideas, but we didn't know how to piece it all together. We didn't want a home divided into lots of little rooms. We didn't want any of the chapel windows to be split up. We wanted a big hall, without it being vast and echoing. We wanted to create movement round the chapel without putting in multiple stairs, which would be incredibly expensive. Creativity was what we wanted the help on. We wanted an architect to have the ideas.'

Below: Roderick James and his team of craftsmen at Carpenter Oak planned and prepared Denys and Marjorie's timber frame before it was delivered to the site

Below and bottom: Architects' models are invaluable in the way they help you visualize the project. Sarah and Jeremy made a model of their house and office for a lecture, while David Sheppard's model of the chapel helped Jane and Gavin understand his plans better.

Developing the Ideas

As you talk with your architect, your original ideas may be modified or transformed into something quite different. The original sketches will be overtaken by more formal drawings and plans until finally the technical drawings are prepared for the building inspector. As this process goes on, it's only too easy to lose track of what your home's really going to be like. Architects' plans are not very user-friendly and unless you are trained to read them or have a good spatial imagination, it may be impossible to envisage the finished building properly. At the very least, colour in the drawings. However, your architect may be able to prepare 3D illustrations or make a scale model, which will make things clearer still. Don't underestimate the value of this. If all else fails, make your own by sticking the elevations and floor plans on card and cutting them out and joining them together. This will help you to understand how your home is going to work in terms of the sizes and relationships between rooms. It's vital that you have a proper grasp of what you've commissioned before it's too late!

Budget

The other thing it's essential to be clear about at this stage is the budget, which to some degree will dictate the size of the house and possibly some of the materials used. There's no point in going for everything you want if it's obvious at this stage that you're going to have to cut it all back later. Without an idea of what you're willing to spend, an architect is completely at sea and can hardly be blamed for indulging their fantasies and coming back with a design that includes every state-of-the-art convenience, when your dream home was something altogether more modest or traditional.

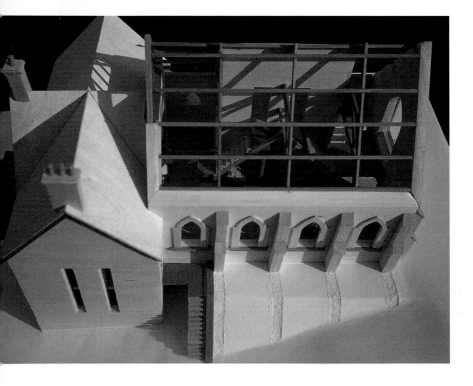

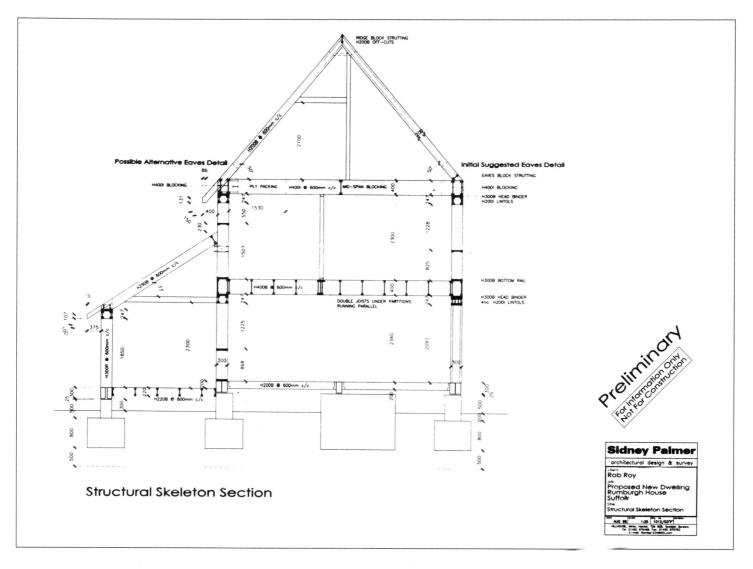

Structural Skeleton Section

Possible Alternative Eaves Detail

Initial Suggested Eaves Detail

RIDGE BLOCK STRUTTING
H200B OFF-CUTS

EAVES BLOCK STRUTTING

H400I BLOCKING

PLY PACKING   H400I @ 600mm c/c   MID-SPAN BLOCKING

H400I BLOCKING

H300B HEAD BINDER
H200I LINTOLS

H300B BOTTOM RAIL

H400B @ 600mm c/c

DOUBLE JOISTS UNDER PARTITIONS
RUNNING PARALLEL

H300B HEAD BINDER
4no. H200I LINTOLS

H200B @ 600mm c/c

H220B @ 600mm c/c

Preliminary
For Information Only
Not For Construction

Sidney Palmer
architectural design & survey
client:
Rob Roy
job:
Proposed New Dwelling
Rumburgh House
Suffolk
title:
Structural Skeleton Section

Who's in Charge?

Another aspect of concern is that once the architect is appointed you may lose control of the project. Frankly, that is up to you but you must make clear the extent to which you want to be involved from the outset. It's important to set up a dialogue between you and your architect so that you can talk freely about what you like and don't like all the way through the process. This communication is essential if the project is to come off. But do listen to your architect because there's a trade-off to be had. Only you know what you want and you must make sure you get the things that are important to you, but their ideas may prove to be a better way of achieving them than yours.

Some people, such as Michael and Lindsay, choose to leave it almost entirely to their architect to come up with something appropriate that can be the grounds for a discussion. Lindsay said, 'Funnily enough, I'm very reliant on the architect. I learned when we did our chapel conversion that the architect felt it was his place to create the interior as well as the exterior, that it was part of his job. We argued long and hard over that, but now I've come round to his way of thinking and I do

Above: The architect's blueprints give the technical specifications, which can be hard for non-professionals to understand. However, they are essential when you are dealing with the building inspector and when the job is tendered to a number of contractors. (*For information only, not for construction.*)

believe that in a way it's his house as well as ours. Maybe it's because he's in the family, but I do trust him.' They left the design completely up to Colin, who produced three quite different designs, from which they chose one.

But they were not the only ones who trusted their architect implicitly. As we've seen, living such a distance from Chilsworthy chapel, Jane and Gavin had to be extra diligent in choosing an architect who they could trust to look after the job, since they would only be able to be on site two or three times a month.

At the opposite extreme is Rob, who knew precisely what he and his family wanted. So he had to work at a relationship with Neil Winder: 'He was uncomfortable about the fact that I'm a unique client in that I take so much hands-on responsibility and have so much input. I think he had difficulty with that at the beginning because it could compromise his professional situation. So much of the success of the project depends on personal chemistry. I know a lot of people who use architects at arm's length. With our level of involvement we needed an architect who could cope with that.' Eventually, having taken Rob and Alida's very defined brief into account, Neil brought round his drawings to find a rapturous reception: 'It wasn't a quantum leap from what we had done. He had taken our elements, rearranged them, added a few things and come up with something that we think is perfect. That's what an architect should do.'

Below: Colin used computer graphics to show the interior of Michael and Lindsay's house in an easily recognizable form.

What Else Can an Architect Do for You?

Another thing an architect should be able to do is to roll with the punches. There's no doubt that the design of most of the houses in the series was modified as building progressed. This could be due to an unforeseen disaster or nothing more than a simple change of mind. The design for Michael and Lindsay's house was constantly in flux as Colin believes that architecture benefits from constant reconsideration and late changes give life to the design. David Sheppard, the architect for the Chilsworthy chapel conversion, also believes flexibility is key, so that if an unexpected problem arises, the design can be adapted and improved.

You may not be as quick-thinking as Tim and Julia who, when the pallets carrying the reclaimed bricks

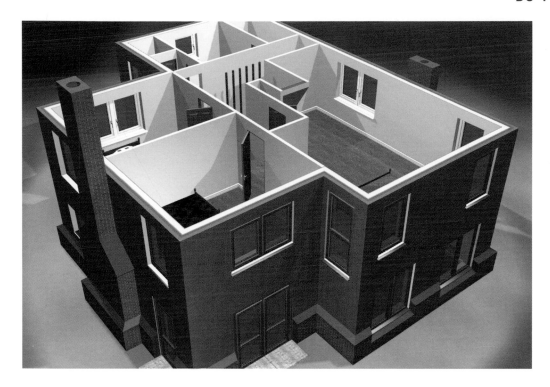

destined to be two fireplaces cracked in half leaving piles of broken bricks, took the opportunity to abandon one chimney stack and have patio doors in its place! But, as Julia subsequently remarked, 'It was obvious that the best views are from here and the light coming in is lovely, so it suddenly seemed silly to brick it up. I wonder how many houses are completed exactly the same as the original drawings?'

But the architect will do far more than just design the house. Once the plans they have prepared have been returned with planning permission, they will work to include any modifications demanded by the planners. Detailed plans for building regulations approval will be submitted by them. They will also prepare specifications for tender so that, with materials specified for every part of the building, all the builders are working on a level playing field, estimating for the same thing and unable to take shortcuts on the bits that you don't see! When the prices come back from the various tendering builders, they will assist in finding ways of cutting back to get the price down to somewhere within your budget. Michael and Lindsay decided that they would rather have a slightly smaller, but identical house in terms of quality than shave off parts of the design to get the cost down. The only major thing they've lost is the swimming pool, which was always a bit of a dream.

An architect should also be able to recommend other specialists who you may need to employ if your building is something out of the ordinary. For instance, both Michael and Lindsay, and Sarah and Jeremy employed planning consultants to help them negotiate the labyrinthine world of planning permission (see Chapter 5, Get Planning, pages 92–109). If there are concerns about the eventual cost of the

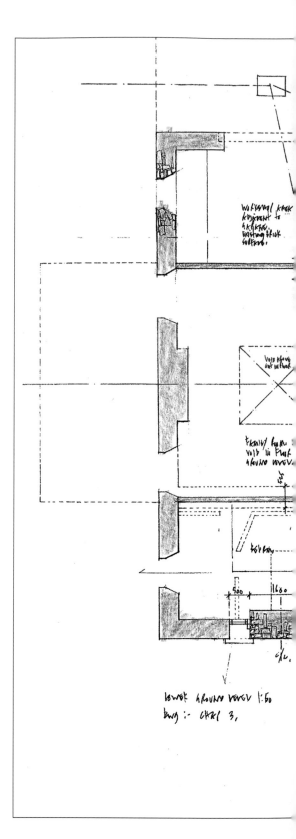

Right: David Sheppard worked with horticulturalist Roy Cheek on the design of the 'heavenly' garden in the Chilsworthy chapel conversion. Using the original architect's drawings, Roy was able to show how he envisaged the plants in the context of the building. (*For information only, not for construction.*)

project, you may want your architect to recommend a quantity surveyor, who will go through the materials you are going to need in detail and cost it out for you. If you're building something original, using huge spans of glass or metal for instance, your architect should also be able to recommend a structural engineer, who has a more specialized knowledge of structures and will be able to advise on the materials you'll need. Had Tim and Julia used a soil engineer, they might have avoided the unbudgeted expense of having to re-dig their foundations to be much deeper as specified by the local council's building inspector.

The architect is therefore in a position to make your ideas happen and to solve any difficulties that get in the way of achieving your goal. You should expect them to be creative, even inspirational, organized and, if necessary, a buffer between you and others involved in the project. And, of course, they should always retain a respect for the kind of building you are aiming for, otherwise you've chosen the wrong person.

The Architect's View

Perhaps the time has come to spare a thought for the architect. What do they look for in a good client? Seeing and understanding the relationship from their point of view may enhance the chances of your own success. Each of the different architects who were working for clients in the series had their own priorities. Neil Winder, who was responsible for the design of Rob and Alida's eco-house, believes clients

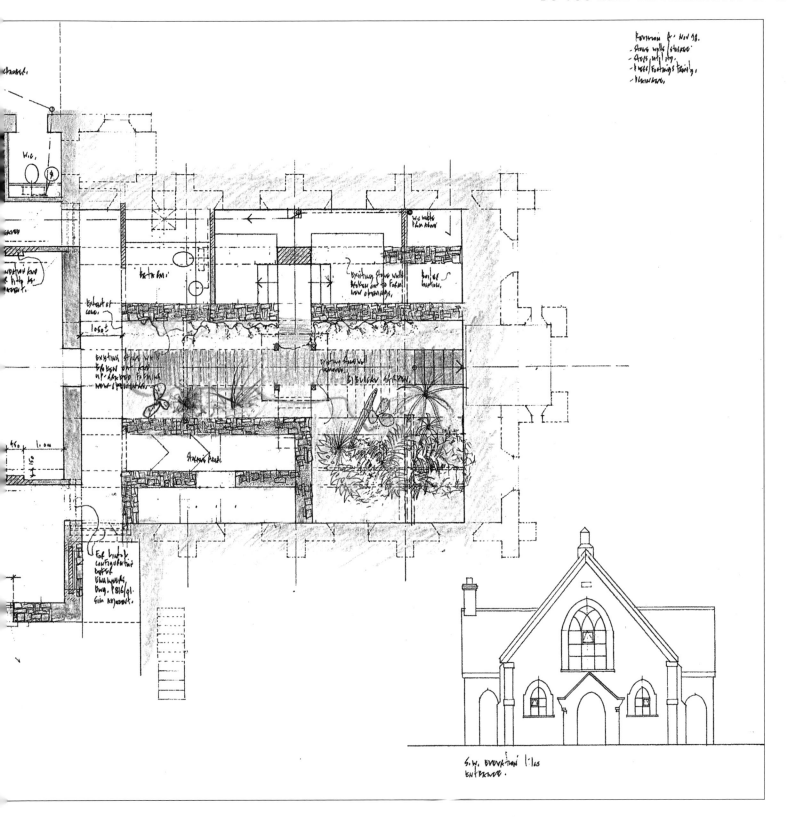

'need to be open and to know their commitment to the project. Often they start with enthusiasm and don't appreciate that their role isn't just planning and design, but they must meet deadlines and pay fees when necessary. They must be there and be responsible at the right time.' Robin Hillier of Architype, who designed the houses put up by the Hedgehog Housing Co-op, feels: 'a client must have a clear

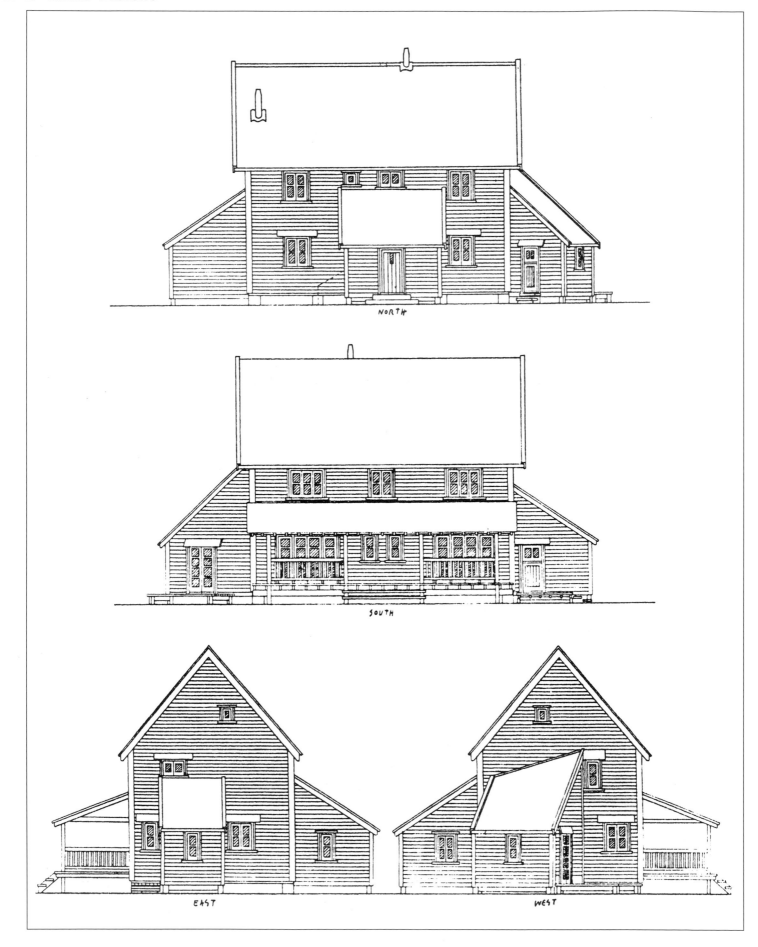

NORTH

SOUTH

EAST

WEST

idea of their requirements but be honest and open-minded about how those requirements can be achieved, and have a recognition that the construction process involves an element of risk.' David Sheppard, architect for Jane and Gavin's Chilsworthy chapel, prefers: 'someone who's very enthusiastic and encouraging because there *will* be problems. They need to be sympathetic to the professionals involved and pay money at the right time.' Roderick James, architect for Denys and Marjorie, likes: 'someone who's enthusiastic, flexible and cheerful. You have to be able to get on together. There's nothing worse than designing a house for a gloomy client. I also like clients who want a bit of a contemporary edge to the building and who are prepared to have their boundaries pushed, but equally I like them to be prepared to push our boundaries too and stretch us a bit.' The things Colin Harwood, designer of Michael and Lindsay's modernist Doncaster home, wants are: 'Wealth! Clients who trust the architect and respect him enough not to try and get off without paying him half his fees.' In short, there seem to be three main characteristics that architects look for in a client: open-mindedness, honesty and enthusiasm.

Other Options

If, for whatever reason, you're still determined not to use an architect, there are other routes. The most hair-raising of these is to do the whole thing yourself. With little or no experience the process will inevitably take much, much longer as you find your way through the intricacies of design and build that others take for granted. You may expect to save money by doing it yourself, but it will almost certainly mean that you'll end up spending more on the oversights and problems that occur along the way, and having many more headaches. Not least, you may discover that you lack that one vital talent in the process of visualizing and then realizing your building – a spatial mind.

You could use a surveyor but they are generally not trained to conceptualize about space in the way that an architect has been. Alternatively, you could use an architectural designer, who will be able to draw up your plans but because they are untrained as an architect, they may not be able to cope with either the structural or financial sides of things as well as you might like. Architectural designers tend to be better at making the bones of the building look good, while the architect can also make the bones work. Of course, there are exceptions, but whoever you decide to choose, always check out their credentials and their previous work first before engaging them.

Opposite: An architect can provide elevations of your house similar to these provided by Neil Winder when designing Rob and Alida's eco-house. They give your fantasy a realistic shape. (*For information only, not for construction.*)

Design
for Living

3

Now the fun begins. With a site and an architect in your pocket, it's time to get to grips with the detailed design of your home. During this process, try to keep a reasonably cool head on your shoulders and don't necessarily be seduced by current design fashions. Be aware of what you're doing and who you're doing it for. In the end, you're the one who's going to have to live with those fashions, not your architect, so be sure their appeal will last for you.

Below: The flexibility of the Walter Segal system means that, unlike most kit homes, the interior can be modified to suit your needs.

Think too about how long you're planning to live in your new home because a prospective buyer may not be so rhapsodic about the more idiosyncratic features you've introduced and you may be disappointed by what they're willing to pay – and so may your bank manager!

Where Do You Start?

First, ask yourself the question – who am I? To achieve the home of your dreams, you need to look at the kind of person or people you are and to be realistic about your lifestyle. Question how much space you really need and decide what it is that you want to do with it and how best to divide it, if at all. Do you prefer a more traditional arrangement of small rooms with separate kitchen, dining room and sitting room, or do you want something more modern, where light and space are the key components of the design and the daily living spaces are contained in one area? Will you be working at home? Where will the children keep their toys and do their homework? Do you enjoy entertaining? What special hobbies would you like to accommodate?

Now, go through every kind of room you could possibly need and decide which are musts, whether you need more than one of them and whether one space can have more than one function. The main rooms to consider are the bedrooms, bathrooms (would you prefer a separate toilet or do you need any bathrooms ensuite?), living room, kitchen (including a separate utility room if you prefer), dining room, study and children's rooms. Other possibilities are a conservatory, cloak-room, garage and porch, as well as considering whether you want a useable attic space. And before your budget disrupts your fantasies, you might as well go the whole hog and think about including a bar, swimming pool, hot tub, sauna, gym, snooker room, wine cellar, stables, dark room or library.

Whittle the list down to what you need and can afford. But remember that one day

Below: Andrew designed an open plan living space for his family that was separated from the enclosed courtyard by a glass wall, making it easy to keep an eye on the children when they are playing outside. (*For information only, not for construction.*)

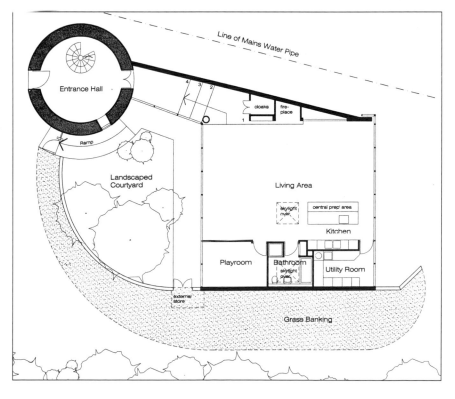

Above: The great joy of building your own home is that you can include whatever features you like in the design, such as this bar planned and now enjoyed by Denys and Marjorie.

you might inherit that unexpected windfall, so there's every reason to provide for future development where you can. If you feel that the attic could eventually be put to good use, make sure that your roof is made with attic trusses that are heavier and more expensive than standard factory-made trusses and which, unlike them, do leave a space that you could convert later on.

Michael Hird and Lindsay Harwood's budget dictated that they scale down their original plans, but there's still space for a pool in the basement. Similarly, architects Sarah Wigglesworth and Jeremy Till and have had to put on hold their sliding, satellite guest room that would have run along the garden wall and docked onto a lobby: 'We've decided to build the basic volume and get as far as we can, then put the other bits in later.'

It's important to look at how the different rooms will relate to one another within the overall design, in terms of both size and position. For example, there's no point in being able to seat twenty in the dining room if your kitchen's so small that you can only cater for six at a time. Neither is it a good plan to have the two rooms at opposite ends of the building. Think of all the fetching and carrying, and how congealed the food will be when it gets to the table. This may sound obvious, but it's a principle that you must consider throughout the house. Even if your space is uncluttered and open, it will work best if it is divided up into areas for different activities, so think about what those activities are likely to be and how the areas within the space will need to relate to one another.

Every home needs a heart or a focus, so decide what and where it is to be. Perhaps the central focus will be the family kitchen, or a huge log fire in the sitting room. Whatever you choose, watch how you organize the rest of the space around it. If you're a multimedia family, you'll need to incorporate the television (or televisions) and hi-fi speakers into the scheme and (particularly if you're working from home) work out exactly where the phone points are going to go and how many lines you are going to need so that you can surf the Net or teenagers can talk on the phone all night without jamming up the only available line.

Lighting

Other important features to consider are electrical and lighting sockets. Lighting is crucial to the final look of your home, since it will show everything off at its best (or worst) and can be used to transform the most unexcitingly furnished room into something romantic or exotic. When planning your lighting schemes for each room, think about the activities that will take place in it. The more multi-purpose the room, the more flexible the lighting needs to be. A large living area will be harder to light effectively than a bathroom, but if you follow some simple principles it shouldn't be too difficult. There are five main kinds of lighting to think about in your home.

- ambient lighting – background lighting which, strictly speaking, should not have any recognizable source.
- task lighting – allows you to see what you're doing more clearly without glaring into your eyes (e.g. a desk light, reading lights or lighting over a kitchen worktop).
- accent lighting – highlights a particular feature, such as a painting, plant or bookcase.
- kinetic lighting – moving light sources that introduce an element of life into any room – open fires, candles, lit fish tanks, even televisions.
- decorative lighting – this form of lighting really only twinkles, but you'll need ceiling fixtures for any chandeliers that, incidentally, can be used as a device to add focus and balance in the centre of a space.

If you can organize the lighting well in advance, then when it comes to moving in, you should have sockets in all the right places. You can also consider a wall-socket circuit devoted entirely to table lamps, switched from a conventional light switch. There will be no need for wires to be trailing around the walls because you didn't think things through properly earlier on.

Above: Position as many windows as possible to the south of the building to benefit from maximum solar gain. Natural light may not always be enough, so you'll need to consider lighting schemes to complement it.

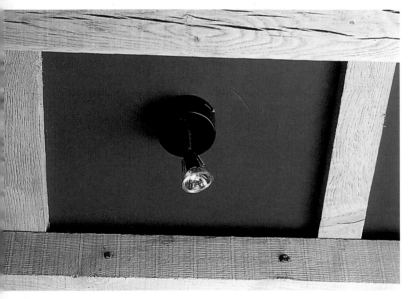

Above: Plan ahead and decide where your lighting will be so that the house can be properly wired before the plasterer finishes the walls and ceilings.

Above right: If you're building your own home you can put lights wherever you like – even in the floor, as Denys and Marjorie did in their atrium.

Opposite: If you've got a favourite picture, think where you're going to be able to hang it. Here Denys and Marjorie's papyrus hangs neatly between the beams.

What Do You Need From Your Home?

Look at the house you're living in now to see which aspects of it could be improved and then included in your new home. Sarah and Jeremy wanted to bring their house and office together. Although they had already worked from home in their previous Victorian terraced house, this time they wanted a properly and efficiently designed office space in their home. They allowed for only two bedrooms since they don't have children and, because they are both academics, they planned a splendid library tower topped by a reading room rising from the essentially open-plan living space. 'It isn't open-plan in the classic manner, in that it is open but there are moments when you can get quite secluded within this great hanging roof.'

The ethos behind the Hedgehog Housing Co-op self-build was inevitably quite different, principally for the simple reason that it had to cater for a small community. Together with their architect, Robin Hillier, they set out to provide a design framework that would allow an ecological approach to construction, as well as reflecting their needs and aspirations. Robin wanted to present an alternative approach to mass housing on a small scale. As such, they agreed that the design would be deliberately 'in your face'. They wanted the final buildings to enable low-cost living, but to combine everything that people should have – such as views and outdoor and indoor living with light – to create useful and flexible spaces. The Co-op wanted to avoid using non-sustainable materials and processes if they could help it. It was also important that the houses could be easily adaptable so that members wouldn't end up living in identical houses, but could tailor each interior to their own style.

Tim Cox and Julia Brock designed their house very much as an expression of the way they live: 'We don't stay indoors much so the ethos was a house which it was as easy as possible to spill out from. That's why we've got the decking outside and so many doors. It's a very child-oriented place and reflects our life of games for the childen and the grown-ups really.' Their ground floor is a huge room, with one end devoted to the kitchen and a long table, with a large sitting area at the other end focused on a large brick fireplace. Wherever you are in the room, you're always aware of the outside and how easily accessible it is. The doors lead out directly on to heavy decking made from reclaimed railway sleepers, which visually echo the tidebreaks way down on the beach below.

When working with Denys and Marjorie Randolph on the design of their home, Roderick James wanted to achieve a building that had a contemporary spin to it.

Below: Internal walls, such as this one between Denys and Marjorie's two bathrooms, can be made of glass bricks which make the most of the natural light available.

'It definitely had to have space and light, and Denys and Marjorie had their particular requirements: the bar, the study, the library, the bathrooms, the way the rooms linked together and the way they used them. They wanted the natural materials as a major part of that. We also wanted to create a lot of different areas outside. If you walk around the house, you'll find it has a completely different feeling from whichever side you view it. When you first arrive and view it from the end, it looks really quite small, but from the back it's got quite an imposing dramatic impact. On arrival, you don't really see what happens beyond the house but once you go in, you're presented with an incredible view. So there's an element of surprise and adventure, which we were trying to build on.' Denys and Marjorie were practical in remembering that this is their retirement home and they have echoed the design of their previous house, where the bedroom and bathrooms occupied the ground floor, as well as the living areas. They have always insisted on a bathroom each. The rooms are almost mirror images of one another, except that Marjorie has the hot tub and Denys the sauna! The large glass atrium forms the heart of the house, where they live and eat, with the kitchen leading off on one side and the bar and Denys' study on the other.

When Rob and Alida Saunders worked on the design of their house they had both been struck by the feel of their architect Neil Winder's home, which is very open, and full of light and colour. They wanted the same effect in their house so they worked together on a design that would use plain materials in a simplistic way to create what would first and foremost be a welcoming family home. The ground-floor living space is principally split between a large kitchen and a big living area, while upstairs two of the four bedrooms will have platform beds, giving the children maximum useable floor space. This arrangement is one that is commonly chosen by people for family life and, together with the rejection of formal living spaces, such as dining rooms, it is becoming a template for family living in the next decade or so.

Michael knew that he required something unique that wouldn't snuggle anonymously beside its neighbours. He wanted a modern house that would make a statement, designed along the lines of those built by Frank Lloyd Wright and his followers. His choice of building style reflects his attitude to life: 'I like having things that are original and unique, whether it's a piece of art or our own house.' For Lindsay, the kitchen is the most important room in the home, so it was the first room that they planned in any detail. The central island has a granite work surface and contains the hob and sink. Otherwise, everything except the oven is hidden in the larder, which has an automatic roller door, operated by a flick of the finger.

The couple wanted the house to be essentially minimalist, with vast open spaces on the ground floor and modular spaces on the upper floor. Colin, their architect, wanted to achieve 'an air of opulence brought about by the space'. No quarter is being given to their two children, Max and Linden. 'We believe that children can get on in whatever surroundings they've been given; they adapt.'

Above: American architect Frank Lloyd Wright's design for the house, Fallingwater, provided one of the inspirations behind Michael and Lindsay's ultra-contemporary home.

Special Features

Do you own anything that you would particularly like to display? Or do you need space to house something, such as a grand piano or a snooker table? It could even be something more mundane that has a particular resonance for you. Part of Sarah and Jeremy's inspiration came from the elegant beech refectory table, at which they had both worked, entertained and slumped over breakfast, in their previous house. 'There's a room between house and office, which is for the table – the genesis of the whole scheme. Sometimes it will be a conference room and sometimes a dining room, so it celebrates this table, making it into the centrepiece of the house.'

Similarly, Michael and Lindsay have a huge Victorian chandelier that they bought from Bradford Conservative Club. It will hang in a specially designed space next to the sweeping main staircase: 'In a sense, it's rather like an art gallery, juxtaposing "baroque" with crisp, modern white walls. It was a question of rising to the occasion not by blending in, but by contrasting the two.'

Making the Most of Your Plot

Take a long, hard look at your site. It's essential to make the most of it. Where are the best views? If they can be seen from upstairs, consider putting the living rooms up there and giving over the ground floor to bedrooms and bathrooms. The previously existing bungalow on Denys and Marjorie's plot had a conservatory that faced north towards the road. Although constrained to build on the original footprint, they have turned their house so that the principal views, most particularly from their atrium, sweep across miles of countryside towards the Chiltern Hills.

Every room in Tim and Julia's house (except the bathroom) looks out over the spectacular south coast seascape. 'The worst drawback is that from dawn there will be at least one white triangle of a sail and we're having to look at them from the land!' This deliberate arrangement of their windows also means that the radio mast

Below: Catching a view like this takes good luck, good design and perseverance.

close behind the house cannot be seen from inside. Similarly, the large windows of the Hedgehog Housing Co-op houses all face out over the roofs of the houses below them and across to the other side of the valley, while the sides and backs of the buildings have much smaller and fewer windows.

In which direction does the site face? Rob and Alida wanted their eco-house to face true south so that they would benefit from maximum solar gain, putting the corridor and rooms that don't need heating on the north side of the building. Large glass windows and a wide, sheltered verandah are positioned on the south side. However ecologically minded you are, it certainly makes sense to orientate the living areas of your house towards the south so that, apart from any solar gain, you can also enjoy the privacy of a sun-filled garden.

Environmental Considerations

What impact is your building going to have on the local environment? If it is in the Green Belt, an Area of Outstanding Natural Beauty or a conservation area, you may want (and the planners almost certainly will insist on this) to minimize the impact. This can be achieved by restricting the height of the building, as both Denys and Marjorie and Tim and Julia were constrained to do. Planting a screen of trees is something that nearly always finds favour with the planners. The Hedgehog Housing Co-op have planted a generous hedge below their houses, while Michael and Lindsay had to propose a substantial tree-planting plan to find favour with the planners, who originally wanted them to build a high wall against the main road to keep their ultra-contemporary house out of sight and presumably therefore out of mind.

The Hedgehog Housing Co-op went a step further, wanting to make 'minimal environmental impact'. Their timber-built houses are in full view from the other side of the valley, but what are seen are the natural 'sticks' of the extending verandahs, balustrading and pergolas, while the pitched roofs are turfed to camouflage them against the hillside behind.

Being only too aware of the sensitivity surrounding his plans to develop the Coleshill water tower, Andrew Tate took the local landscape very much into consideration. 'The land immediately adjacent belongs to Three Valleys Water and they have two great big reservoirs semi-buried in the ground. However, they sit about 3.5 metres (11½ feet) above the ground level and they've got grass banks and grass roofs on top of them, so they're disguised.' Using this as inspiration, his one-storey extension to the tower is similarly hidden from the road; a turf roof extends into a grassy bank leaning against the outside wall which sweeps round to create a hidden courtyard. This is an ingenious solution to the problem of how to discreetly site his building.

Some people feel less constrained by the desire for invisibility or conformity. This is often dictated by where they build. It might be hard to justify putting Michael and Lindsay's modernist house in a rural retreat of thatched, stone-walled cottages, but in their desire to make an individual statement and their belief in the intrinsic style of their project, they have been lucky in finding an appropriate site on the fringes of a major town, where they are surrounded by different architectural styles. You may find that applying for planning permission to build a striking or avant-garde design on a brown-field site is easier than on a green-field site or in a conservation area.

Consider the impact your home may have on your immediate neighbours. After all, these are the people beside whom you're going to be living for some time. They have the right to formally complain to the planners about any aspect of your design

Below: Denys and Marjorie were inspired by the sense of light and space in Roderick James's previous work.

(see Chapter 5, Get Planning, pages 92–109), so don't deliberately antagonize them. Within the constraints of the plot, Colin Harwood carefully sited the modernist truncated diamond-shaped house as far away as possible from its 1930s neighbour in Doncaster.

Local Agenda 21

The 1992 Earth Summit in Rio produced Local Agenda 21, a 'programme for working towards sustainable development (meeting people's needs and improving the quality of life without damaging the environment), which will take us into the next century'. However, much of the work needed cannot be carried out without the co-operation of local government. Chapter 28 of the programme asks all local authorities to develop a local strategy for achieving sustainability, i.e. Local Agenda 21. Many issues are involved, but among them is the need to look at local elements of vernacular design in the face of the onward march of developers, who often put up buildings without a thought for the local environment.

Until recently, the prevailing opinion was that to be good, architecture had to be grand, but now the value of lowly architecture is being recognized. When designing your new home, it's important that you look at its surroundings and identify what is particular to them. If you are looking at a building for conversion or a community with a strong historical and environmental context, then it's important that your own building should reflect that through the use of the right tiles, real stone, local colours, the slant of the roof, the style of doors and windows, and so on. All these things matter enormously if the identity of individual communities is to be perpetuated.

Sustainability of materials and usage is a key element in Local Agenda 21 and these issues are covered more widely in Chapter 8, How Green Can You Go? (pages 146–161). Incidently, the term 'sustainable' as referred to in Local Agenda 21 also covers the sustainability of a community.

Converting Buildings

When converting an old building, be it water tower, chapel or barn, the constraints are manifold. Not only must its situation and the needs of the people who will be living there be considered, but so must the building itself. You need to be sensitive to its construction, its history and, most importantly, its feel. The main thing that attracts people to barns as possible homes is the sense of scale and space. And the combination of timber with the shape of the barn frequently makes it a wonderful

framework in which to build a home. To get the most from it, it's best to keep it as open-plan as you can. If you effectively construct a traditional house within the framework, you lose the soaring height of the beams and the unique sense of space, both of which made the barn so special in the first place.

More difficult still is the conversion of a church or chapel, buildings that generally have a much colder feel, although with a similar sense of space. One of Jane Fitzsimons and Gavin Allen's main concerns in converting Chilsworthy chapel was to remain sympathetic to the building, although its size presented problems.

The first task for their architect, David Sheppard, was to come up with a design that would somehow exploit the space in the vast roof area and the considerable basement, while acknowledging the stunning views and the fact that Gavin and Jane were adamant that they didn't want the floor levels to cut across the large windows. They wanted five bedrooms (with one independent from the rest, for

Above: Converting an unusual building is an exciting and challenging task. But it can also have its limitations, as Andrew found when his freedom of design was restricted by his desire to keep some of the industrial metal features in the Coleshill water tower.

visiting relatives), a well-equipped study, which would eventually enable them to work entirely from home, and a family room. But they didn't want to lose the sense of space that had attracted them to the building in the first place. The major problems identified early on were designing a way to get up into the roof space and how to use it, while retaining the grand scale of the building. How could the stairs and the different floor levels be designed to achieve this?

David reinvented the aisle (the major axis of the building) as a staircase, which divides to follow the minor transverse axes and so becomes the major structural element in the space. 'The ratification of the stair was the most difficult thing to do. Where do you step off the landings in relation to the windows, floor levels, etc? So I spent a lot of time defining what the staircase would look like within the volume and the movement of people up and down it. Then I introduced an internal garden which utilizes about one third of the basement area in the corner of the building. On entering the building, you immediately walk around the garden perimeter and on towards the dining/living area, which faces out across the valley.'

In David's design this open-plan area is interrupted by a well in the floor, which looks down to the family room below, inspired by Jane's throwaway request for a

Opposite: The vast interior space of the Chilsworthy chapel gave David Sheppard plenty of scope for imaginative design.

Below: It's hard to imagine a 'heavenly' garden rising from these ruins at Chilsworthy chapel.

dungeon for their new baby, Sam! Above, the bedrooms and study were carefully positioned to fully benefit from the massive windows.

The Outdoor Spaces

What about the space outside your house? Is your TVR going to be housed as spectacularly as its owner? If so, will the garage be an integral part of your building, or will it be separate, and where will it be? Give a thought to the rest of the space available in a garage. Is it practical to use the roof space for storage or as a playroom? If there's not any room to spare and there's nowhere to put your tools, think about whether to include a tool shed in your plans.

Denys and Marjorie had their large tool shed completed before the house. This meant that not only could they provide security for some of the site machinery, but they could also open it for their first tool-shed-and-caravan-warming party when they moved on to the site for three weeks of summer 1998! Any pressure in Tim and Julia's house has been eased by buying DIY store sheds for the girls, to which they can escape and where they can keep their bikes safely locked away.

And the garden? Most people tend to turn a blind eye to it until the building's up and they've moved in. They've far too much on their plate without having to plan anything more and they baulk at the idea of additional expense. Besides, it's hard to imagine a building site as a flourishing mature garden. But when is the appropriate time to consider its future?

Rob believes that because the house is an integral part of its environment, the garden should be designed simultaneously. He has planned theirs on a permacultural basis: 'We've designed systems so that they are sustainable, yet do what they're supposed to in the most efficient and economical way. It's a question of placing the elements in a way which minimizes the amount of energy needed by maximizing the interaction between them.' For example, the ducks are housed by the pond, the fruit cages and the vegetable beds, because they love eating slugs.

In terms of their own needs, Rob and Alida wanted a recreational all-weather surface for the children and a system of lawns that would make up little private areas for Alida's 'haven', a meditation area, and so on. The cold frames, herb spiral and log store are conveniently situated near to the building and great thought has gone into what you will be able to see from the house. For instance, Alida's 'haven' is hidden from the study by a bank made from the earth dug for the foundations.

Similarly, Jane and Gavin thought well ahead and employed horticulturalist Roy Cheek, who planned both their internal and external gardens. Inside, the inspiration for the garden came from the staircase, which rises 'almost like Jacob's ladder' to the ceiling. Roy planned that the ascent would be through a semi-transparent cloud of greenery provided by three varieties of tall and arching small-leafed bamboo. 'Scent will pervade the air from a few carefully chosen plants, such as white angel's trumpet and jasmine, which will climb the underside of the steps. Similarly, a few others will provide intriguing dashes of colour (lavender-blue passion flower and primrose-yellow mimosa), yet will not overpower the green cloud effect. Down in the well there are evergreen ferns and blue streptocarpus. I'm trying to create a heavenly feel.' The key to the design has been 'maximum effect for minimum effort', so the plants are evergreen and don't need endless maintenance and tidying up.

Outside, Roy has kept the feeling very simple, using two Irish yews (for Jane's Irish ancestry) on either side of the door, with two white standard roses between them. On the right side of the chapel, the predominant colours will be greens and yellows (including a Killarney strawberry tree), while on the left, the colour theme will be silver-grey green and purple using herbs, with a purple lily palm giving height. Roy likes to link the gardens he designs with his clients, so not only Jane's but also Gavin's ancestry will be represented, this time by a Cornish orchard with old varieties of apple and cherry trees.

You may not have such a precise idea of what you want for your garden, but as you're going to have the builders in, decide early on whether you want a terrace or a barbecue area. Marjorie knew she wanted a terrace with a pond and lots of potted plants, and Denys had his heart set on a lake to one side of the land in a wild flower meadow. The couple sought advice from the National Trust to find out the best way to create one, aware that it would have to be carefully managed. They agreed that they wouldn't know exactly what they wanted nearer the house until they'd settled in and could sit in their atrium considering the space around them.

Michael and Lindsay had an idea of what they might achieve too – a pond that would reflect the trees as you gazed on it through the sitting room window, but overall something quite minimal with some natural sculptures and perhaps some topiary. 'But these things evolve. You can have as many plants as you like, so we've decided to wait and see what it looks like.'

Having worked out what it is that you want from your house, the way in which it will meet your needs, the overall feel that you want it to have, you also need to consider carefully the materials that you will use to achieve it (see Chapter 4, Material Facts, pages 72–91).

Material
Facts

4

Apart from the spatial and ergonomic design of your home, the other obvious way in which your surroundings and their aesthetics will affect you lies in your use of materials. These aspects of space, use, materials and finish are of course inextricably linked. So, at the same time as considering what you want from your home, you need to question what materials you must use to achieve it. Some systems, such as traditional post-and-beam timber construction, dictate the interior and exterior aesthetic of the building. This is the case, for example, with the green oak in Denys and Marjorie Randolph's house and the softwood construction of Segal houses. Other systems such as brick and pre-fabricated timber-panelled structures (such as Tim Cox and Julia Brock's house) leave no trace of their identity on the internal faces of the building and so don't impose any kind of aesthetic stamp on the interior design.

Apart from catering for your own tastes, it's imperative to consider how your proposed building will fit in with its surroundings. Of course there are sites, both in the countryside and in towns, where sensitively designed modern architecture may fit in, but in conservation areas it is unlikely to be welcomed, as in Denys and Marjorie's case, where the choice of materials was closely scrutinized by the local planners. They will attempt to exert their influence and use legislation and procedure to persuade and ultimately dictate your choice of brick, the pitch of your roof and the tiles that you use. But it's up to you to decide whether you can make a convincing case for building something that's out of the ordinary – if that's what you want.

Sarah Wigglesworth and Jeremy Till's, and Michael Hird and Lindsay Harwood's urban sites border on conservation areas, where the concern was that the appearance of their proposed homes might offend those living nearby and, more importantly, could compromise the integrity of a community of buildings and weaken their importance as good local and historical examples. This is a very touchy issue that has been well-publicized by Prince Charles's plain speaking on a number of building proposals. Others inevitably feel strongly opposed to those theories of conformist design. Colin Harwood, who designed Michael and Lindsay's Doncaster house, feels that the only way forward in the development of urban architecture is by accepting a mix of old and new: 'The beauty of British cities is the complete mish-mash of different styles all living together which shows how cities grew. It's fundamental to British cities that we're allowed to juxtapose brand spanking new with old.'

Bricks

They say that every man's home is his castle and there's no doubt that the majority of people in this country still prefer living with the sense of solidarity and permanence afforded by bricks and mortar, as indeed they have from Roman times. The earliest bricks were hand-made and sun-dried in Egypt and Babylonia in ancient times, but it was the Romans who introduced them to this country, where they have been used with varying enthusiasm ever since. Despite a heyday in British brickbuilding during Henry VIII's reign, when rapid advances were made with

Below: Denys and Marjorie chose to combine bricks and rendering for the external finish of their house.

wonderful feats of ornamentation, bricks weren't adopted widely, either socially or geographically, until the Industrial Revolution. Before then, brick buildings possessed local characteristics, which harmonized with the land on which they were built and from which they materialized. But with the advent of the mechanization of processes formerly done by hand and the proliferation of the railways and canals, costs fell and bricks were easily and more cheaply available throughout the country.

Then, earlier this century, the concept of the cavity wall was

introduced whereby, instead of building a single wall of bricks and mortar (which scarcely protected against cold and damp), two walls would be raised, the inner load-bearing one built with cheaper bricks. Between them lay a cavity through which damp could not pass and these days it is used to hold additional insulation. This is still the way most houses are built in Britain.

If your home is surrounded by other brick buildings, especially in a conservation area, it is quite possible that you will be asked to use the same brick, although there may very often be a cheaper and almost identical alternative. There are two types of brick. Stock bricks are made of good-quality clay and look good on the outside. These can vary in price depending on where they've come from and the care that's been taken in their manufacture. On the other hand common bricks are made to less high standards and are used in places where you can't see them.

Alternatively, there are breeze blocks or lightweight 'blown cement' blocks of varying kinds, which again are generally used where they're not seen. Sand-faced flettons, which consist of a particular facing on one side of a common brick, give

Below: The oak framework ready to be delivered to the Randolphs' site.

you the look without the expense. Certainly, nowadays there is an infinite variety of brick and tiles available, and their careful use and combinations of style and colour, with their different effects, can transform a rather ordinary exterior design into something much more interesting and attractive.

Despite an abiding attachment to brick in Britain, there is a move towards using materials such as timber, earth, straw and even cob (mud and straw). Concern for the environment means that some people want to build their homes from renewable resources. In addition, these alternative materials connect us to the past because of the largely rural traditions from which they derive and they can be effectively utilized in a wider context today.

Above: Masonite is a pre fabricated material composed of wood particle board and is produced in the north of Sweden.

Timber

Wood has universal appeal, despite being used far less often than brick and block in this country. Its appearance, its feel and its comforting creaks all go towards making it a fantastic material to live with. Wood has the effect of making us feel relaxed, reassured and secure. It has been used in the construction of houses from time immemorial and offers many practical advantages to the self-builder, as well as having enormous aesthetic appeal. Concerns that it is a fire hazard are quite unfounded. In fact, wood burns steadily with a protective layer of charcoal forming round the outside. It is therefore quite possible to calculate the necessary size of beam that will remain strong for an hour or so of burning, allowing time for the occupants of the house to escape.

Timber-panel buildings tend to be what the many package companies provide in kit form. The inner load-bearing wall is fabricated off site and can be erected very quickly. This involves fewer people on site and can avoid brickwork and the use of wet trades, plasters, mortars and concrete (except for the foundations and any plinth platform the building may have). Most frequently though, the outer skin

Right and below: The Segal method starts as a wooden post-and-beam structure. This use of wood is one of the most attractive features of the Hedgehog Housing Co-op's houses.

is built with brick and block, giving it the appearance of something more conventional. However, it can also be timber cladding, which was what Tim and Julia chose. The range of houses built this way is phenomenal. You only have to look at one of the self-build magazines or to visit one of the national or regional self-build shows to get an idea. They range from unimaginative pastiche Tudor to contemporary American beach-style homes. In Sweden, IKEA is even selling its own flat-pack homes made from wood.

Tim and Julia needed their house fast. Their cottage was too cramped for the six of them and Julia was expecting their baby, which they desperately wanted to be born in the new home. Apart from the weatherboarded beach hut look that they were after, timber could also provide the advantage of speedy construction. The inner wall of Tim and Julia's house was up in a matter of days in April 1998, with the roof going on shortly afterwards. Unfortunately, Tiger wasn't born in his new home but none the less it only took five months before they could move in.

The Segal Method

Wood is also cheap, pleasant to handle and relatively easy to use without needing expensive machinery and skills to craft it. In the 1960s, the architect Walter Segal pioneered a method of building that used a simple post-and-beam (or post-and-rail) technique, planning the house round the size of the components. The lengths of timber could be bought off the shelf, brought to the site and put together with the minimum of cutting and fitting. This obviously means there's a minimum of wastage, which is a cost advantage. This system needs few foundations since the posts rest on concrete pads and these stilts make it ideal for a sloping site. The positions of the windows and doors fit within the grid of posts and beams, as do the internal non-load-bearing walls. It is relatively straightforward to put together and doesn't require the traditional skills normally associated with house-building.

The Hedgehog Housing Co-op in Brighton is composed of seventeen people, many of whom had no previous experience of construction work, but still proposed to build their ten houses themselves. They chose to use a design based on the Walter Segal principle, which has meant that they have been able to achieve the results they wanted with the minimum of outside assistance.

Denys and Marjorie also watched in amazement as their oak barn frames were assembled and raised: 'It's the original pre-fab home, like Meccano!' Their home uses the time-honoured post-and-beam technique favoured by Walter Segal, but originally invented by thirteenth-century barn-builders.

Top and above: With the right materials, an essentially functional feature such as this wooden peg in Denys and Marjorie's roof can have a design value of its own.

Rob Roy was closely involved in the building of his eco-house. With five skilled friends, he succeeded in running and participating in most of the build, despite never having had any previous building experience. His build utilizes the 'stick' method: walls are constructed flat on site from 'I' section Masonite beams, a green product whose shape gives you the insulating void in a wall. Construction is with a hammer and nails and so quick that Rob's entire house, minus the cladding and the roof, was up in a couple of weeks. The 'stick-built' method is not post-and-beam, rather it is a home-built version of the timber panelling construction that Tim and Julia opted for. As such, it too has a minimal impact on the interior aesthetic of the house.

Ecological Advantages

When considering materials for their ecological value, timber must come out on top. Sourcing materials locally is an important green issue and timber is an ideal solution. If it is locally available then very little energy will be needed to get it to your site. At the moment Britain imports well over eighty per cent of the timber it uses, although the Forestry Commission is working hard to counteract this, having doubled the amount of forest cover in Britain over the last 100 years. Timber can be grown 'sustainably': the annual amount harvested does not exceed annual new growth. It has low embodied energy (the energy used to produce and transport a product to site), is extremely energy-efficient and can provide excellent insulation. Wood is also durable and requires a low level of maintenance. One downside is that timber buildings heat up quickly but, unlike their concrete or brick counterparts, they do not retain heat in the walls so they cool down quickly too. Nevertheless, it was the only serious option open to Rob and Alida when designing their eco-house. Masonite joists are a Swedish pre-fabricated product composed largely of wood particle board similar to hardboard. Rob also chose green larch weatherboarding for its weatherproofing qualities, with Scandinavian softwood windows and reclaimed wood floors throughout.

Earth

Going underground or using the earth to shelter your home is not as avant-garde as it perhaps sounds at first. People have been living and building underground or partially underground for thousands of years, from Paleolithic cavemen through to the extraordinary pre-Christian underground settlements in Kamalki and Derinkuyu in Turkey, Chinese underground communities and cities, and the

Victorians and Georgians, who frequently built basements in their houses, or the bunkers used to shelter civilians during the air-raids of the Second World War.

The revival of earth-sheltered housing began in the 1970s and has since been developing round the world. It comes as an answer to the global energy crisis, the ever-rising population density and pressure on space. Earth-sheltered housing provides low visual impact, low maintenance costs, stability in temperature levels (it is warm in the winter and cool in the summer), and protection from extreme weather conditions. Rather than a primitive method, it has developed into a very sophisticated technology.

The British Earth Sheltering Association was founded by three architects in 1983 to encourage the design and construction of such buildings. A number of homes using earth-sheltering techniques now exist in Britain. In the 1960s, architect Arthur Quarmby built his own home, aptly named Underhill, in the Peak

Below: Paul Sant designed The Set, an underground farmhouse in Maes-y-Coed, Wales.

District National Park, Yorkshire. More recently, David Woods has designed Rabbi Jonathan Black's house in Hertfordshire, which is entered by steps leading down from two glass pyramids to rooms built round two courtyards. Mole Manor in Gloucestershire is another example, carved into a hillside and based round a central atrium, lit naturally through a dome at ground level.

Simon Ormerod surreptitiously built his underground house on land he owned just outside Wadebridge in Cornwall. Having lived there for seven years, first in a showman's wagon and then in a self-built chalet, he acquired a camouflage net, brought materials to the site in his Land Rover and organized lorry deliveries by night. It took six months to complete without anyone – including the planners – realising. More recently, the MP Bob Marshall-Andrews has had a holiday home set into the top of a cliff in the Pembrokeshire Coastal National Park. While causing some local controversy, he is thrilled with his 'elegant cave', which commands breathtaking views out to sea.

Pierre d'Avoine was another architect we started following in the series. His plan was for a small house in a west London suburb, built underneath his garden. Unfortunately, due to planning delays we weren't able to see his story through (see Chapter 5, Get Planning, pages 92–109). To carry off the design he will need to call on the benefits of twentieth-century materials too. After digging the hole and removing the earth, the external shell of the house – made of steel sheet piling – will be dropped into place. 'It's all dry construction, which can be fabricated off-site and is very fast to erect. Internally, there's heavily insulated stud partitioning lined on the inside with plywood. The floors are timber, with perimeter heating in a trench by the windows disguised by a grille. The wooden flooring carries on into the courtyard as decking.' Underground homes don't have to be damp, dark burrows – with clever use of light and space they can be made to feel as pleasant as any above ground.

Turf Roofs

One feature of earth-sheltered houses that is transferable to those above ground is the turf roof. Renowned for their insulating properties, they have been used, among other places, on Scottish crofts and the traditional flat-roofed buildings of Scandinavia. Sarah and Jeremy planned a wild meadow of poppies and cornflowers blowing in the long grass and perhaps even some strawberries on their roof. The Hedgehog Housing Co-op has researched shallow-rooted plants and are growing various aromatic herbs on theirs, while Andrew Tate is using the turf to hide away

Opposite: Underground homes don't have to be dark. The interior of Mole Manor in Gloucestershire is lit by a domed skylight.

Above: Turf roofs are attractive, ecologically sound and easy to build and maintain.

his family's living quarters. Given modern materials such as butyl rubber sheet, turf-roof technology is not difficult to get right.

Straw

Another material that has been used in building for some time is the straw bale. The three little pigs immediately come to mind but perhaps the first little pig just didn't build it right! People have used thatched roofs here for many centuries but using the straw as a wall took longer to catch on. The first straw bale houses originated in Nebraska, USA, after the introduction of horse- and steam-powered mechanical balers in the 1840s. It was only a short time before farmers used the resulting big building bricks to make temporary shelters on the prairie. When they realized how well the shelters stood up to the weather, these original pioneers rendered the buildings against damp and pests, and began to use them as temporary housing. The first recorded building was a schoolhouse in Bayford,

Nebraska, in 1886, with simple churches and houses following. From then on, the craft developed until substantial and sophisticated buildings went up, which remain standing today.

The predominant concerns about straw bale houses have proved unfounded. These included worries that it is a fire hazard but the straw is packed so compactly that not enough air circulates within the bale to encourage combustion. Another worry is pests, but if properly protected, there's no more danger of rodents or pests getting in than in an orthodox house. However, damp and mould are a major threat to straw bales, but if they are rendered with a 'breathing' plaster of lime or mud, or protected in some other way, it shouldn't occur provided the bales are raised more than 15 centimetres (6 inches) above the ground with a moisture barrier between them and the footing.

Although straw-bale houses are being built all over the world, in Finland, Russia, Canada, France and Mexico, they have got off to a standing start in Britain – until now. Barbara Jones runs a Yorkshire construction company, Amazon Nails, and is currently pioneering the method over here: 'Straw bale frenzy is a disease sweeping the country! It's accessible so it means people who haven't been able to build their homes now can. It's cheap; it's a lot of fun. It uses sustainable materials which are readily available in Britain. The designs are very straightforward so you don't need to use professionals who charge very high fees.'

Barbara has been involved in constructing a number of buildings, including a beautiful circular house in Clones in the Republic of Ireland, and another, more conventionally shaped, in the Brecon Beacons National Park. A straw-bale garage workshop, planned to become a living space, exists in north Yorkshire but otherwise the buildings in Britain, such as an environmental centre in

Top and above: The straw-bale house built in Clones by Amazon Nails.

Gloucestershire, a forge near Newcastle or a community office for a Belfast school, have so far only functioned as work spaces.

Straw Bales in North London

Sarah and Jeremy have used straw in their technologically innovative building in north London – how much further can you get from the rural plains of Nebraska? Jeremy feels that many of our ideas of what constitutes the urban environment basically derive from the nineteenth century, so what he and Sarah are contributing is something which is 'not another pastiche in a mish-mash of brick and render.' They have designed their office and home using materials which are outside the normal canon of architecture and building. As academics they are naturally driven by theoretical interest, but the building is also intended as a prototype that is acceptable today. 'The range of materials that people consider for building nowadays is surprisingly limited. This is not just a straw-bale house – it's more to do with the use of different materials.'

The couple chose to use a heavyweight construction for their office, which rests on gabions (stone-filled cages that are seen on the side of motorways) filled with recycled rubble. 'It is labour intensive, messy and slow in the way it's put together. But it has advantages because a heavyweight building evens out temperature shifts and has a much slower response time. It's quite stable in its feel and has good accoustic properties. Facing onto the railway is a wall that is made of sandbags. A bit of cement goes in with the sand so that over twenty years the bags will disintegrate and eventually will leave a concrete wall in the profile of the sandbags.

'We wanted to make the rest of the office out of cast iron – the equivalent of Aga doors – but

Below: Sarah looks at her future walls!

that would have been desperately expensive and heavy. Instead, it is made out of padded waterproof fabric so looks like a duvet. It's an example of taking a domestic technology and using it in a building.'

The house itself has a timber frame and is of light construction and that's where the straw bales come in – all 700 of them. The rest of the building is steel-framed and raised from the ground on steel columns, which regularly punctuate the open space of the living area, while two of the external walls are made of straw. The interior will be rendered but outside on one wall they will be protected by a transparent plastic waterproof shield so the hairiness of the bales is left visible. The fourth, south-west wall is completely glazed, apart from a pod on the corner which contains a bench seat, which pops out through the wall onto the terrace.

Sarah and Jeremy have had to be careful to prevent the house from overheating, so they have designed a series of canopies above the level of the windows, and vertical fins with sliding shutters, both of which will shade the interior and prevent it from getting too hot in the summer, yet open it up in the winter. The library tower is exposed steelwork infilled with bookshelves, while the exterior larder wall is rendered.

Cob

Another ancient tradition that has seen some revival in this country is the use of cob walls, which are made from a mixture of mud and straw. Bob Bennett, an expert in the restoration of historic buildings, has built a house from scratch in Beaulieu Forest, where it's now used as an educational centre. In the Middle Ages men built with the material immediately available to them. If you got up at dawn and, with other villagers, raised a house on common ground before dusk (to include four walls, a roof and a fire in the grate), then you were allowed to keep it. Bob decided to see if it could be done with twenty-five helpers, using original tools and even dressing up in appropriate period costume for the occasion.

There is a lot of restoration work taking place in this country on old cob houses and even a few new ones or add-ons are going up in Oxford and the West Country, including a cob bus shelter. In Bob's opinion. 'They're ecologically sound because all the material they're built of is reusable and they're better insulated than modern houses today. Lime plaster and lime render lets buildings breathe so the atmosphere inside them is far, far healthier. He is supported by Peter Bryant, who restores Devonshire cob houses and lives in one that is 700 years old: 'It's magnificent, full of character and history, warm and cosy with its undulating walls.'

Above and right: Using age-old working methods and dressing up appropriately for the occasion, Bob Bennett and his team of helpers built a cob house in a day.

Glass

Glass has become almost synonymous with modern twentieth-century building techniques. All over the country, glass conservatories are proving to be a successful way of extending a house. With the manufacture of glass with increased spans, it can now be used as a structural element in a building and work as a wall. We're familiar with the sight of office blocks that appear to be made of nothing else, but the use of glass in a domestic setting is only beginning to find a foothold.

In London's Islington the elegant brick frontage of a quiet four-storey Victorian terrace is interrupted by the glittering façade of a house designed by Future Systems, whose external walls are entirely made of glass. Of course, two walls of Andrew Tate's conversion are glass to let the outside in.

Colin Harwood, the architect for Michael and Lindsay's Doncaster home, has used vast areas of glass that reach from the ground floor to the roof: 'I really love the juxtaposition of very modern materials and modern shapes with really old-fashioned things like Lindsey and Michael's chandelier.'

The idea that the extensive use of glass will make a building cold is now redundant, given today's sophisticated manufacturing techniques. Glass can be double- or triple-glazed to ensure accoustic and thermal benefits, and can also be chemically coated, which stops heat loss through radiation. It opens your house to the outside world, emphasizing and blending in with the surroundings, it allows a light stream in and has the added advantage of letting the sun heat the inside of the building. Obviously, the question of privacy may have to be addressed with blinds and the practical question of cleaning may pose a few day-to-day problems! But none the less people are now overcoming these concerns.

Below: Lindsay visited a school in Vienna which used the same glass that Colin proposed for their Doncaster home.

Combining Materials

When it comes to converting and restoring an old building, you may not want to stick to time-worn fashions and may well wish to take advantage of what

modern technology has to offer, blending the two together in a way that will bring out the best in the original, while making it conform to your lifestyle. David Sheppard carefully chose the materials used for the Chilsworthy chapel so that 'the new parts of the building will complement the old and vice versa, respecting the volume and the feeling of the space, while imposing a new element into the building which will give it its new identity.'

David's plan from the start was for the plasterboard walls between the existing timbers to be coloured to highlight both them and the stone walls. Naturally, the most striking thing about his design is the staircase, which is in laminated timber, conceived to look almost as if it's floating in space, while structurally supported by posts at the starting point and the top. Its sides are a series of glass panels topped with a wooden handrail: 'The idea is to retain the spatial quality but give it a degree of transparency so it looks like a piece of sculpture in space.'

In the case of Andrew's conversion of the Coleshill water tower, he took enormous care to preserve the integrity of the original landmark building. Built in 1915 by German prisoners of war, the red-bricked tower is topped by a steel-plate water tank surrounded by decorative cast iron bracketry and balconies. The only substantial change to the fabric of the tower is the reinstatement of the bricked-up windows. However, the new single-storey extension takes advantage of modern materials rather than echoing the brick appearance of the tower. Two walls are

Above: The careful use of glass can light up your home, as Denys and Marjorie's gallery shows.

Opposite: This house in Islington, designed by Future Systems, is an example of a contemporary building that uses vast spans of glass in its construction.

Opposite: The Chilsworthy chapel was originally built using locally quarried stone.

made of concrete poured into insulating polystyrene blocks (Becoform), one of them banked up with earth. The remaining walls are glazed. This way, together with a skylight, the extension will be bright and light, with constant reference to the world outside. It will also be hidden by the two bunker walls and earth-sheltering bank on one side.

Wood possesses tremendous aesthetic qualities and it can be effectively used with other, more modern materials. Roderick James, architect for Denys and Marjorie's house, has combined the classic style of an old oak barn with a contemporary design for modern living: 'I think the combination of oak and glass contrast with each other. You've got this wonderful transparent material, which is very smooth and hard and clean, against something which is organic. If you use oak in a slightly different way it acts as a reference point to the past. You can get away with doing things in a far crisper way once you've got some of the familiar warm materials in the house which do make it homely – which is, after all, what you want in a house.'

When considering design, do give thought to the door and window frames. These are, after all, among the first things you see when you come to a house and they really can define its appearance. Your concern should be with their shape – there is, of course, a huge choice when it comes to windows – and also the material they're made from. Most people still prefer timber but if you're pressed for time, as Tim and Julia were, or want a maintenance-free existence, you may opt for uPVC, although these frames don't have the same effect and they certainly won't meet with the approval of the eco-lobby. Similarly, give due consideration to your roof. It can be made of anything from tiles, slates, and aluminium to shingles and turf, but again, make sure that it complements the body of your house.

On a practical note, whatever materials you decide to use to express your way of life, it pays dividends to obtain samples beforehand and to look carefully at how they will sit together, otherwise you may find that the house in your mind's eye becomes an eyesore in reality. If you are in any doubt at all about one of the component parts, get hold of as many samples as you can to ensure that what you are going to have to live with is exactly what you want and properly matches the look and feel of the rest of your house.

Building materials available today encompass an extraordinary range, whether natural or man-made, traditional or contemporary. These, married with simple or sophisticated building techniques, can be used to create a unique place that you can really call your own.

Get Planning

In 1947, the first Town and Country Planning Act was introduced. Its aim was to contain and control development of housing after the Second World War when a great deal of cheap housing was going up indiscriminately throughout the country. As a result, every district council now has a planning committee made up of a number of councillors whose job it is to consider, approve or refuse all planning applications submitted, observing the recommendations made by their planning department and consulting the Unitary Development Plan (UDP), a statutory document drawn up to ensure they can't act merely on whim.

When an application is received, the neighbours, the highways and drainage authorities, your parish council, local amenity groups and, if you're proposing alterations to a listed building, English Heritage and other amenity bodies are notified and invited to comment. The planning officers, who are trained and qualified in the planning field (unlike the councillors, who make up the planning committee), assess the applications and subsequent objections, with or without your involvement, and finally write a report that recommends acceptance or refusal by the planning committee. Occasionally, if the plans conform to the local planning policies and are not controversial, if the planners are recommending acceptance and if no objections have been raised, they can make a decision without referring matters to the council. This is known as using 'delegated powers'.

Planning permission is not concerned with the structure of your house, nor with the land on which it is to be built, but with how it will fit into the surrounding environment, whether a change of use is involved, how it will affect the density of population and other similar issues. For example, the officer will want to look at

the siting of your building, its compatibility with neighbouring buildings, the materials you propose to use, access, whether it falls within a conservation area, and so on. When Denys and Marjorie Randolph approached their planning officer they were told that in an Area of Outstanding Natural Beauty their new bungalow had to occupy the footprint of the previous one, although its floor area could be enlarged by fifty per cent, and that all materials would have to be approved.

The local planning files are accessible to the public so it is quite possible for you to see what planning permission has been sought, accepted or refused in the area, and maybe even on your own plot. This will give you an idea of the pitfalls that may lie ahead and you can gauge how clever, confrontational or, if you're lucky, how supine you may need to be.

Above: Caught between two very different architectural styles, Sarah and Jeremy were lucky to get their neighbours' whole-hearted support.

Overleaf: Obtaining planning permission on a virgin coastal site is virtually impossible. 'Bungalow gobbling' or bungalow demolishing is a great way of getting permission to build on the site of your dreams.

Having found your land, you will know which kind of planning permission has been granted on it. The different types of permission are:

- outline permission – this lasts for three years and means the land has been approved in principle for development.
- approval of reserved matters – this follows the submission of detailed plans for your building.
- detailed permission – this is effectively the first type plus the second and lasts for five years, by which time work must have started: a single footing (foundation trench) with a building inspector's approval should be sufficient.

Do not buy land without either the first type or the second. If your heart is set on the place and you are convinced you can win the planners over, take an option, as Andrew Tate did, until you have, preferably, the third type. You cannot build a new building or carry out a substantial conversion without it.

Applying for Planning Consent

It's worth remembering that anyone can apply for outline consent on a piece of land, provided the owner is aware that it's happening. The consent is given to the land itself, not to the person making the application nor indeed to the landowner. Check how long any existing permission has to run. If there's already detailed permission for a house unlike anything you've ever dreamed of, you can always reapply with your own design. But make sure the outline permission is current. When Tim Cox and Julia Brock bought their land at Newhaven, the planning permission for a modern four-storey house had lapsed. They took the calculated risk that given once, a plan for a similar-sized house would find favour again. Luckily, they were right.

The paperwork is straightforward. For outline permission, the planners require a location plan (from Ordnance Survey 1:1250 or 1:2500) and an existing site plan, showing any buildings, trees or other site features. For reserved matters or detailed permission, you or your architect will also need to provide detailed floor plans (1:200, 1:100 or 1:50), elevations of the front, back and sides of the house (1:200, 1:100 or 1:50), details of the materials you plan to use and a proposed site plan with the footprint of your building clearly marked, showing the access route and any trees that may need to be felled (1:500 or 1:200).

Send the planners the specified number of copies (never fewer than four, but it could be as many as twelve), together with the detailed application form and the standard fee, both of which you will find out about at the local office. Officially, the decision should be reached within eight weeks, but often it takes longer. The planning officer must visit the site after permission has been sought, but he is not obliged to discuss anything with you before putting in his recommendation and can refuse point blank to enter into any conversation, however casual, about your ideas. Thankfully, most planning authorities realise the benefit of dialogue and officers will usually talk to you.

But don't just sit back and wait for the planning office to reply. There may be plenty of things that you can do to influence the final decision, particularly if you are building something unorthodox. And don't think you have to wait until you have submitted the plans. Rob Roy and Alida Saunders knew that their proposed eco-house might meet with opposition since it didn't echo the buildings in the immediate vicinity, although it was to be timber-built and similar to a weatherboarded Suffolk barn in appearance. 'We contacted the planning officer responsible for this area, who agreed to meet us on site. I talked to him about all the details of ecological building and he said he couldn't see any problems. I worked on a relationship where I would contact him if I needed to bounce any ideas off him. I can't recommend enough that that's what self-builders should do. That way we were able to respond to problems before we got to the planning meeting. For example, the original design had the garage on one side and the entrance on the other. The Highways Authority were objecting because it was too close to the corner, so we just flipped the design over. In the end the planning committee itself was totally in line with the different sustainability design features and accepted the design as it was.'

Similarly unorthodox were Sarah Wigglesworth and Jeremy Till's plans for a house with a contemporary look, constructed from materials not normally associated with urban building, perhaps most particularly straw bales. It was to be built at the end of a Victorian terrace in north London. The couple knew their plans were controversial so they deliberately adopted tactics that they felt would ensure permission was granted. They decided to employ a planning consultant. Gamekeepers turned poachers, planning consultants usually have a background in town or country planning and have the advantage of understanding exactly how planners work, how to communicate in their language and how to navigate the most arcane elements of planning control.

Above and right: It's impossible to second-guess the planners. Who would have expected them to give the go-ahead for this incongruous Thames-side penthouse.

Opposite top and below: Even if it is very different, the planners may welcome a contemporary design if it blends in with the surrounding buildings, as the architect David Wild's house does in London

Overleaf: Sarah and Jeremy never expected this design to be so readily accepted by the planners. (*For information only, not for construction.*)

'We took a fairly high-risk strategy in that we deliberately didn't have any negotiations with the planners at all. With our planning consultant, we put together a twenty-page document which covered every single point of Islington and national planning legislation, and basically gave the planners the argument as to why they had to give us permission. It was very persuasive. We also did very full drawings, not hiding anything, and we just sent it in.'

Sometimes it pays to use a scaled-down model of the build but when, about three weeks before the submission, Sarah and Jeremy showed their consultant the rough model made partly from pan scourers used for a lecture they were giving, he went white. 'He obviously had no real idea what kind of building he'd

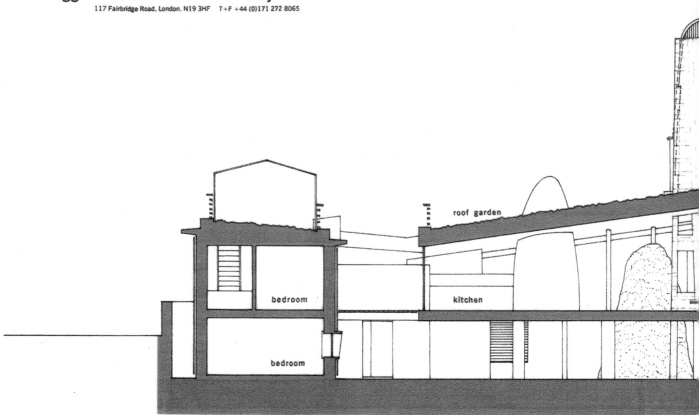

Sarah Wigglesworth Architects + Jeremy Till
117 Fairbridge Road, London, N19 3HF   T+F +44 (0)171 272 8065

roof garden

bedroom

kitchen

bedroom

LONG SECTION THROUGH HOUSE AND OFFICE   1:100

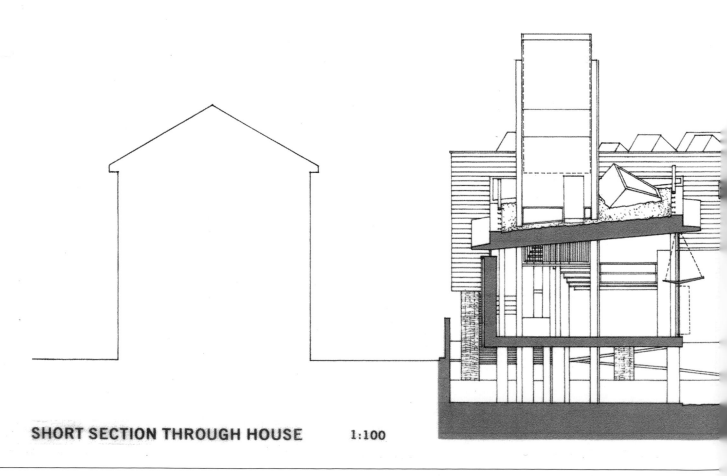

SHORT SECTION THROUGH HOUSE   1:100

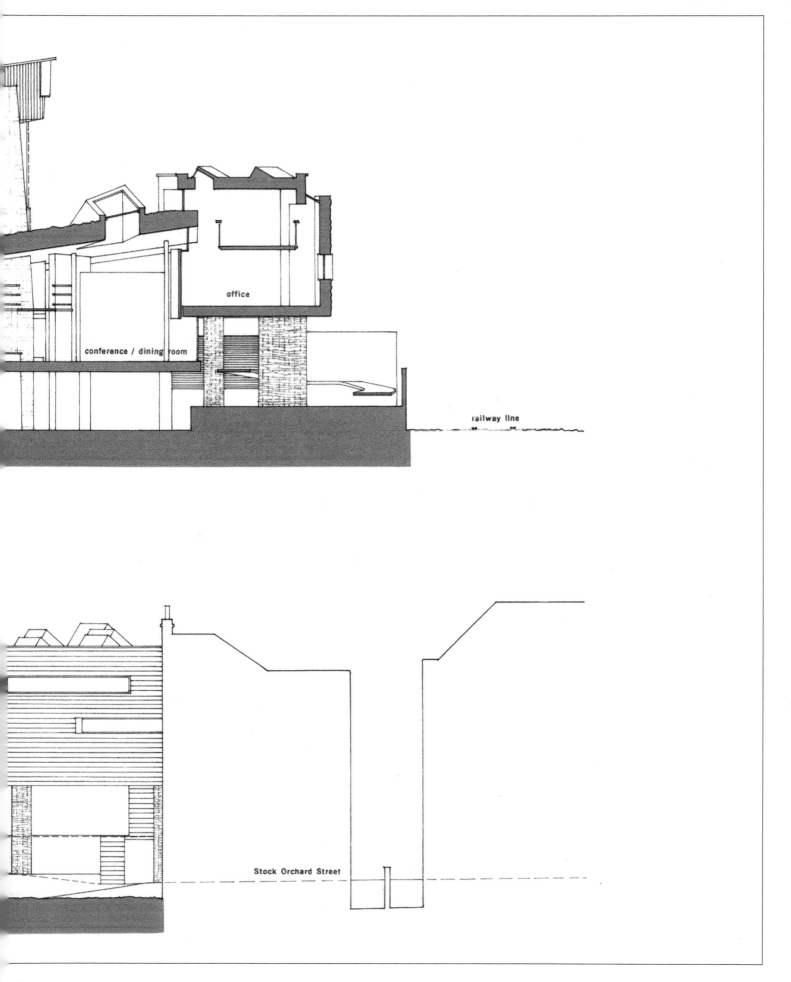

been working on for the last six months. So we decided not to put the model in when we made our application.'

Once you've applied for permission, a period of consultation follows, which Sarah and Jeremy used to their advantage: 'We made a nice white model showing the building in context and wrote a letter to all our forty neighbours, and invited them to an open day on site. We went to Norfolk and brought back twenty straw bales to build a straw-bale wall so that they knew what it looked like and we did some coloured drawings, put the model on a bale and provided wine. What was absolutely apparent was that we could have designed anything we wanted. It was the fact that they weren't going to have a smelly old forge sitting on the site and that we were involving them in the plans for its becoming residential.'

Six weeks later Jeremy phoned the planners to see how their application was being received. 'It was a completely surreal conversation. I asked what was happening and they just said, "Oh, that's fine." And that was it. It was done on delegated powers and didn't even go to council. We'd deliberately put in sacrificial elements, such as the library tower, which we would have happily forfeited to build what we wanted, but it was completely unnecessary. We didn't have to compromise at all.' So those sacrificial elements were included, despite any second thoughts they may have had, rather than reapplying to the planners and rocking the boat.

Andrew and Deborah were to experience quite a different story as they embarked on their battle to secure permission for their proposed development of Coleshill water tower. Despite a huge swell of local support, the planners remained obdurately against their plans. But the couple had been forewarned about the local council's vigilant protection of the Green Belt: 'We decided the best way to deal with it was to win over local support, especially from the parish council. We phoned the relevant councillor and asked if we could meet at the site, when I would show him the coloured boards we had prepared illustrating what we would do. He advised me to convert the tower in a way that wouldn't look too different to anyone looking at it from a distance.'

Andrew's proposal left the exterior of the tower untouched, converting the interior to accommodate bedrooms and bathrooms. More controversial was the proposed new one-storey square extension with its banked side and turfed roof. 'We pointed out that this is a local landmark used by all of Coleshill: it's part of their national history. If our planning didn't go through, what would Three Valleys Water Board do? They'd probably demolish it as a real liability. I think it also helped that we were moving into the village, with the kids going to the village school. We would be becoming part of the village as well. 'We were invited to present our plans to the parish council one dark spring evening. I'd expected to present to a few people over a table, but the place was packed! Suddenly there was a power cut so, as I talked, people had to shine torches on the boards I was using to demonstrate our plans. It was the most dramatic presentation I've ever done in my life.'

Below: One of the drawings Andrew used to convince the parish council that his development of the Coleshill water tower would not disrupt the local environment. (*For information only, not for construction.*)

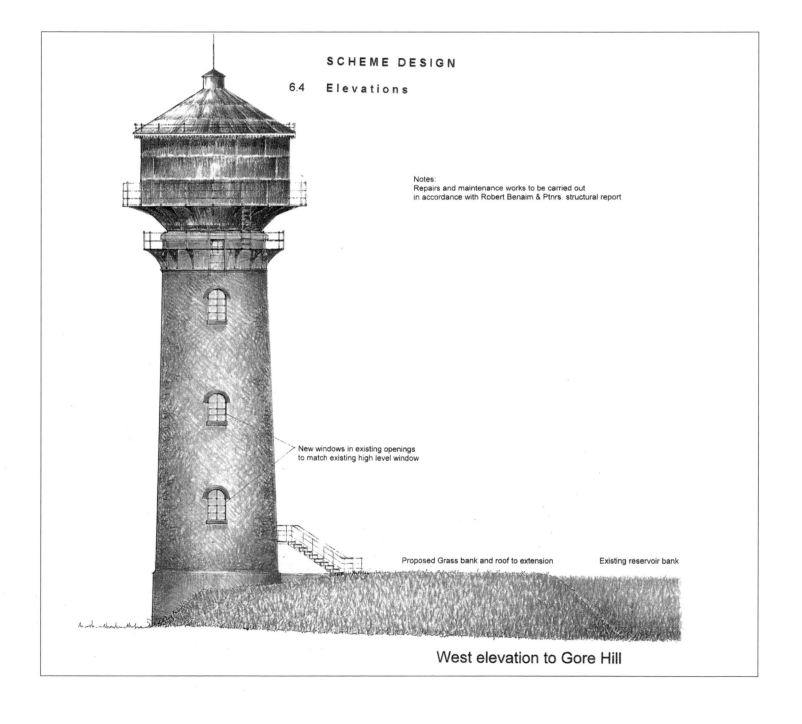

SCHEME DESIGN

6.4   Elevations

Notes:
Repairs and maintenance works to be carried out
in accordance with Robert Benaim & Ptnrs. structural report

New windows in existing openings
to match existing high level window

Proposed Grass bank and roof to extension   Existing reservoir bank

West elevation to Gore Hill

Andrew and Deborah got unanimous support for their plans. When they informed the planners that the parish council was wholeheartedly behind them, their response was that none the less, it remained against policy so they were still going to recommend it for refusal, although they did advise that they should make the application. And that was that. They refused to talk to them further. But the couple weren't going to give up without a fight.

'We put a brochure together demonstrating our plans and the care we were taking to preserve local history, and sent it to every one of the planning committee. We also went to talk to the neighbours, who turned out to be for us, some even writing letters of support. After a week I phoned the committee members and tried

Below: Despite the fact that it was next door to a petrol station, the local planners insisted that Colin Harwood's proposed house should be invisible from the road.

to engage them in a conversation about the scheme to work out how well we were going to do.' Several people, including the chair lady, were effusively in their favour, while others remained vehemently against the idea.

'The committee meeting was nail-biting. They put it to the vote and it was eight all. I looked at the chair lady, who looked as though she could drop through the floor. Precedent dictates that the chair has the casting vote, but that she should follow the recommendation of the planners. They decided to vote again. Someone hadn't voted first time round, but second time voted for us, it was through! The only hurdle left was the submission to the Department of the Environment because the development involved building in the Green Belt, but their permission was received two months later.'

Similarly, Michael Hird and Lindsay Harwood were to meet implacable opposition from the planners for interrupting the 1930s red-brick surroundings with a clean-lined, unorthodox contemporary building. 'Before we bought the land I did find out that it wasn't in a conservation area. But lo and behold, when we went for planning permission they announced it was just on the boundary. Not that it was in it, but it could reflect on it so they would have to bear that in mind.'

Originally, their planning application was turned down because modifications were required – the planners wanted the finish to be brick and not white render, and they wanted a huge wall between the house and the main road so that it could not be seen. 'The planning officers recommended refusal, but the councillors unusually requested a site visit.'

That morning, despite their presence not being officially required, Michael turned up in his old Fiesta van, looking pretty scruffy, and got Lindsay to bring along Max and Linden, their two young children, for the sympathy vote. He'd also asked an old friend, who happened to be a Conservative councillor, for advice on the best political strategy to adopt – which name to drop, and which not!

Colin Harwood had made a model of the building in relation to the surrounding properties, together with a written justification of what they hoped to do. It included a resumé of the building and a review of all the different styles of housing within that area. He also provided a drawing so they could see that nothing of the house was visible if you were walking along the main road into town.

'We weren't supposed to say anything. The council architect did most of the talking, supporting the planners' provisos, but it was clear he wasn't for it at all. My *coup de grâce* was to say that if they weren't going to give us permission, we wouldn't buy the land. I left it at that. They gave the permission, but with the same restrictions as before. We decided we'd got away with quite a lot so we'd better not press the issue.'

For the Hedgehog Housing Co-op it was not the planners but the neighbours – one or two of whom provided ongoing opposition to the scheme even after the permission had been granted – who posed a problem. Its situation was very different from most self-builds in that the local council was already on their side when it put in for planning. But the planners could not ignore the neighbours, who were vociferously against the plans – so much so that it involved substantial additional expenditure in answering their objections. Among other things, they were concerned with the conservation of the chalk downlands, which meant that 900 square metres (2,952 square feet) of turf had to be relocated and watered in elsewhere. A herpetologist was brought in to write a report on the existence of slow worms and lizards in the area, and transport them to a safe place. Archaeologists were employed to excavate the ground to check for evidence of hill forts or previous historical inhabitants, but after digging several trenches they went away, satisfied there was nothing. Because there was a complaint about the scheme being too visible, all environmental sensitivities went out of the window as the level of the land was dug away by 2 metres (6$\frac{1}{2}$ feet) at a cost of £80,000.

Perhaps worst of all was the initial hostility, which even involved threats to burn the houses down as soon as they were built. The way the Co-op reacted was to respond carefully to each query by writing to the planners and, as people got to know them, the atmosphere improved immeasurably. There were frequent meetings between the planners and the Co-op, which more or less successfully thrashed out the issues at stake.

Refusals

But what happens if both planners and neighbours are against your plans and permission is refused? If the local planning authority has failed to respond to your application within the statutory eight weeks (or within whatever longer period may have been agreed), or if they have partially or completely refused the application, then you have recourse by appealing to the Secretary of State. Normally this is done in writing, including all your supporting evidence, and the outcome is decided without the oral participation of either of the parties involved. Don't embark on this course of action lightly: it can be time-consuming, costly and disheartening. If you can keep in conversation with your local planners by reapplying for permission with an amended design, you can make as many reapplications as you want within the time limit of the outline consent. It may save you a lot of heartache, but sometimes the nature of the design can make it impossible to grant permission.

Pierre d'Avoine was dismayed to find that his plans for a virtually hidden underground house in London's suburbia met with no support whatsoever. However, his belief in his project was such that he was not going to roll over and give up. His battle has lasted for over two years, ending up with him having to appeal. This is a high-risk and stressful strategy, and you need to be entirely confident in your arguments in order to win.

'Unfortunately, the neighbours haven't liked the idea at all and that's why we had to go to appeal. They organized a petition objecting to it. So I ended up persuading lots of people to write in its favour, from the Royal Fine Art Commission to the President of the RIBA.

'Some authorities are fantastically good at giving you informal advice, but in this case the Ealing planners didn't want to meet with us to talk about it, before or after I submitted the plans. I didn't have a single point of contact with them. They just turned it down. Their reasons were that it was overdevelopment, sub-standard accommodation and out of character.

'When we went to appeal, we didn't completely win because although none of those three points were upheld by the inspector, he objected that people could stand on one part of the raised garden and look down into the street and, more importantly, look into neighbouring properties. He worded his report in such a way that when we went back to the planners, having lowered that part of the roof, they couldn't refuse us again and they very reluctantly gave us permission on condition that they approved our landscaping and the materials we're going to use.' This was to prove another major delay for Pierre.

Amendments

More often than not, permission comes with various provisos that you will have to observe. Among other things, these may be to do with the siting or the height of your building, access to it, the removal or planting of trees or the use of suitable mains supplies. They may dictate particular materials that you must use in order to fit in with the local vernacular.

Tim and Julia were asked to lower the roof line of their Newhaven house. Having done this, Tim now regrets not having dug the ground floor deeper to accommodate the request. As a result, instead of having three floors, they ended up with two and an attic. They had to forfeit the master bedroom they'd planned on the top floor and, instead, it now occupies the space originally allocated to two of the proposed bedrooms on the first floor.

Despite the fact that the Oxfordshire bungalow they were demolishing had only been reroofed within the last ten years, Denys and Marjorie were asked to use different tiles that would match their neighbours'. 'Hand-made tiles are extraordinarily expensive. We'd taken the concrete tiles off the old bungalow and planned to use them on the tool shed roof. The ones for the house were smaller and a better colour. I took samples of both to the Newbury planning office. They wrote saying the concrete tiles weren't acceptable.'

When Marjorie threatened to appeal, she was hastily transferred to the planning officer's superior, who agreed to a site meeting. It soon became clear that they had not read Marjorie's letter carefully and understood that the couple were proposing that the concrete tiles be used for the house itself! He gave them the go-ahead for use on the tool shed immediately. And the moral of the tale? Fight your corner.

Building Without Permission

What if you do go ahead without alerting the planning authorities? It's not a risk to be taken lightly since it is very likely that they will find out – probably when someone complains or when a planning officer or building regulations inspector just happens to stroll past it. If you don't comply with their subsequent demands for modification or, at worst, demolishment, or formally apply for permission, they can serve an enforcement notice that states what you must do and the date that you need to get it done by. Prosecution can follow, although if you appeal, the notice is suspended until a decision is made.

Should you build a home and somehow manage to live in it for four years without this being discovered by the authorities, the council cannot take action. Similarly, if the building's use has changed or planning conditions have been ignored then, in the unlikely event of your having lived there for ten years without anyone noticing the changes, you're exempt from planning controls.

Building Regulations

But just because the planners have at last given the go-ahead, don't think that it's over yet. You've still got to apply and pay for building regulations through another department of your local council. Application can be made simultaneously to your application for planning permission, but it's more common to wait. With your fee

and application form, you should provide the detailed plans you sent to the planners, marked up with such items as the structural layout, drainage, room and window sizes, insulation and materials. You need to include a plan of the foundations, one or more sections through the house, and drawings of any extra details if necessary, such as the stairs. If your building is something out of the ordinary, you may need to ask a structural engineer to support the structural detail with their calculations.

The building inspector's concerns lie with the structure of the house and making sure that it complies with the Building Regulations Act. They will assess the detailed plans and make sure the work on site conforms with those plans. When the trenches were dug for Tim and Julia's house, they found that the ground conditions weren't firm enough, so the building inspector insisted they dig down another metre (about 3 feet). That, and the problem tree roots, cost an unbudgeted £4,000.

Make no mistake. The building inspector has the power to make you dig everything up so that they can check that the foundations are laid soundly, so don't steam ahead before their inspection. On receipt of your application, you will receive a series of postcards for you to send, when appropriate, to alert the building inspector as to when they need to visit the site. You may find that at the beginning work progresses so quickly that you'll resort to the phone, rather than the cards. Usually, the building inspector visits the site at agreed stages, probably before the foundations are poured, to inspect drainage works and to inspect structural works. When the work is completed they will sign it off. However, they can arrive unannounced just to see how things are going and if something unexpected crops up during the build, you can always ask them to come and advise you.

At last, when the building is finally up and ready for occupation, you should receive a letter saying that, to the best of their knowledge, the works are carried out in compliance with the building regulations and you can be secure in the knowledge that your home is structurally sound.

Planning permission stories are like bad holiday tales – almost everyone's got one – but they all demonstrate one thing: however you choose to manage the situation, don't give up. It's not over till it's over.

Above: Denys and Marjorie were able to use concrete tiles such as these on the outbuildings but not on the house itself.

Money
Matters

6

Of course the crucial considerations in this whole business of self-building are financial. You need to be certain right from the outset that you've got access to enough money to see your building through to the end. When you've calculated just how much you're going to need, then work out where it's going to come from. You may be in the happy position of being able to lay your hands on the total amount in cash, but most people will need to borrow some money in order to bring the equity they have, usually gained from the sale of their current home, up to the level they need.

Before you can approach anyone to ask them for a loan it is vital to plan out your budget and cash flow, otherwise the whole project may come to grief. You need to be confident that you will be able to pay out the appropriate amounts, as and when they are required throughout the building process. Besides, why ever would a bank or building society, housing association or even your great aunt want to support you without some evidence of careful calculations on your part? They all need to be convinced that this is a viable project being run by someone who has every intention of seeing it safely through to the end so that any loan will eventually be recouped with interest. Even if you're in the position of being cash rich, a careful budget is just as essential so that you can see exactly where your money is draining away and whether you need to keep a tighter rein on the build.

Finances really do need to be planned out carefully from the beginning. You may not be as lucky as Jane Fitzsimons and Gavin Allen, who were badly advised when they bought their chapel at auction, but who just managed to save themselves from disaster. Confident that they would easily be able to raise the necessary money to pay off the outstanding balance within four weeks, they were horrified to find that the building societies they approached were not interested in lending it to them. When they had to ask the auctioneer to grant them an extension for payment, he immediately threatened to sue them for interest and damages, but after speaking to their solicitor, he did give them some extra time, which they successfully used to frantically scrape together the necessary money from every possible source.

Calculating the Cost

The big question is, of course, 'How much will it all cost?' Although there are inevitably some imponderables, it is possible to get a fair idea by looking carefully at all aspects. The three areas that need to be considered are the land, the outside costs and the build itself.

The Land

It is impossible to use a rule of thumb when it comes to buying land since costs obviously differ depending on position and location. It is safe to say though that land generally represents somewhere between a third and a half of the cost of the total build. Another vital deciding factor is how badly you want it and how much you are prepared to pay to get it. It is entirely up to you how much you spend, but just make sure you've got enough left over to complete the project. If you are in any doubt over the value of the plot, do some detective work in the area first and find out how much similar plots have gone for. You can also investigate sale prices of local houses that are similar in size to the one you're proposing to build and compare them to your total projected spend. This will give you an idea of whether you're paying through the nose or not.

Asking prices for land, like houses, are negotiable so don't be afraid to begin by offering less. The only dangerous way of buying land is at auction, when adrenalin may get the better of you and, because of a sudden rush of blood to the head, you end up paying far more than you intended. If you're worried about getting carried away, send someone else to bid for you. You may miss the excitement, but at least you won't have blown the building money as well.

Outside Expenses

In your calculations, it's vital to remember the extras that are often far from cheap. First of all, there are the solicitors, who will probably be charging for their conveyancing services by the hour. You can at least be relieved that there is no

Overleaf: English weather is the enemy of the self-builder, as Andrew and Deborah found at Coleshill. Bad weather is one of the many problems that can delay your build and so cost extra money.

stamp duty payable on plots costing under £60,000. Your architect's fees must not be forgotten and neither must those of any related professionals you may choose to employ, such as planning consultants, quantity surveyors, structural and soil engineers, project managers, site managers, and so on. As we've seen in Chapter 2 (Do You Need an Architect? pages 36–53), it's up to you to negotiate how these fees are paid, preferably in a way that suits your cash flow.

You can expect to pay VAT on professional fees, but it's important to check the VAT status of your project: it can be complicated. If you are managing the building process yourself, then you must factor in the labour costs, which you will have to negotiate individually with each sub-contractor. Should you choose to use an architect or one main contractor, they will deal with this for you and the cost will be reflected in their price.

Statutory fees for planning permission applications and building regulations applications will need to be paid, as will the fees for the building inspector's inspections. The latter are on a sliding scale related to the cost of the project, with some concessions for small domestic work. You will also need to take into account the cost of your loan, i.e. the interest rates involved, and the required valuation fees. Andrew Tate and Deborah Mills found it difficult to gain financial support for their water tower conversion until the bank used by Andrew's business came to the rescue. Until then it had cost us a lot in arrangement fees to set up, and they were charging $3^3/4$ per cent above base rate, which is a very commercial rate.'

Mortgage and insurance companies will require structural warranties to reassure them that the building is worth their investment. The architect's final certificate can be used as proof that they are satisfied that the job has been done properly and may be acceptable to your bank or building society. However, if you sell your home, these warranties may not be enough to satisfy a potential buyer's mortgage company. Independent structural insurances that will cover your house, for over ten and up to fifteen years, against defects arising from its construction are offered by NHBC (National House Building Council), FE Wright or Zurich. These organizations have inspectors who will want to inspect the site but, like some building inspector's visits, their arrival will be unheralded. Even if you haven't needed to borrow money to build your house, you will still need these warranties when you decide to sell your house, particularly if your potential buyer is trying to raise a mortgage themselves.

Connections with the major utility services all need to be paid for. Write to your local gas, water, telephone and electricity companies and ask for written quotes first. Remember too that if your site is nowhere near access to the public sewer, you will have the considerable additional expense of buying and installing either a septic tank, mini-treatment plant, cess pit, composting toilet or reed-bed system.

Access to the site and eventually to the house should be allowed for. The builders will need to be able to get heavy machinery and lorries delivering materials as close to the plot as possible. You will not be popular if they block the road outside, either with the builders or your neighbours! If you need to build a driveway, even if it isn't covered with Tarmac at this stage, don't forget to add the cost of this into your financial considerations.

It's extremely important to take out site insurance, particularly if you are doing the work and hiring the sub-contractors yourself. If you are employing a main contractor, it is very important that they have all the relevant insurances and it is down to you to check this for yourself. Insurance premiums can be expensive, so shop around to find the best deal you can, but don't make the mistake of ignoring insurance altogether. The costs resulting from an incident on site could be a lot greater. If you don't feel confident choosing your own policy, an insurance broker will be able to advise you – another fee to add to your budget!

Make sure you check the details of the policy closely to see how long it will remain valid, what exactly it covers (some will cover activity outside your site, provided of course that it is directly relevant to your build) and the indemnity limits. Many insurance companies offer packages especially tailored for the self-builder that contain the three main insurances, described below.

- public liability – This covers you against any claim made by a third party for any injury, damage or loss that has happened as a result of your building works. The fact that they might be trespassing is usually deemed irrelevant. You need this insurance from the moment you buy the land, even more so if there is already a building there, which could be dangerous.
- building works – This covers any damage or loss incurred to the building under construction, to the plant or the tools. It can be incurred by vandalism, fire, flood, storms, subsidence, and so on. For example, machinery was stolen from Denys and Marjorie Randolph's site. Apart from having insurance, they responded by completing their sizeable tool shed well before the house so that there was somewhere for valuable equipment to be stored. If you're using a main contractor, this insurance should be taken out jointly. Theft is obviously a likely risk, but check your policy carefully first

Top and above: To save money, Rob and his family left their comfortable home, shown top, to move into a couple of caravans on the site of their new house.

because you may find that there is an upper limit to the sum insured and there may have to be a separate policy.

• employer's liability – This covers any injury that may occur to one of the labourers on site, including their death. Any main contractor must have this insurance, so don't employ one without it.

Depending on how directly involved you are in your build, you should, as Rob and Alida Saunders did, consider taking out personal accident and health insurance. If you are injured and the works are delayed as a result, the compensation offered by such a policy may help.

Where are you going to be living during the months of building works that must take place before you can finally move in? If, like Denys and Marjorie, you want to stay in the comfort of your own home, it's probable that you will need to arrange a bridging loan with your bank. Beware: this can become horrendously expensive if the arrangement runs on for longer than initially expected. If you find that you can't sell your first home at the right moment, then you may find the costs mounting rapidly and with no end in sight except the bankruptcy courts! If you can do the same as Denys and Marjorie and arrange the sale of your house with an obligingly flexible buyer before you embark, so much the better. They were confident in the knowledge that their daughter and her family were waiting in the wings to buy the house and take over the vineyard as soon as they moved out.

Otherwise, it may be a better arrangement to release your equity by selling your house, as Tim Cox and Julia Brock did, and then move into rented accommodation for the length of the build. At least then you will know that as soon as you move into the new house, any other outside financial arrangements will immediately come to an end.

Less comfortably, but almost certainly more economically, you could choose to live on the site. Having sold their old house, Rob, Alida and their three daughters bought and moved into two caravans at the corner of the site. One held a bedroom for the girls, which Alida was at pains to make as comfortable and homely as possible, a bedroom just big enough to hold a bed for Rob and Alida, and a small shower room. This caravan led into a second one, which contained an office for Rob and a largish (as caravans go) living space with a kitchen. They built a wooden porch onto the front, which acted not only as a place to dump muddy boots and macs, but also as a draught excluder.

Paul Crouch also lived on the Hedgehog Housing Co-op's building site in a Portakabin. While economical, this solution can be phenomenally uncomfortable, particularly during the winter, so don't underestimate the rigours of this option even though it may suit your budget better. And before you move in, remember to get the mains services connected first so that at least you'll be able to wash and go through the bills at night.

Another thing to bear in mind is the security aspect of all this. If you are living on-site, then it is far less likely that you'll be the victim of theft or vandalism, either of which could affect you, if not in terms of direct replacement costs, at least because of the time taken to repair the damage. Make no mistake about this: in the building game, time is money.

Should you decide to either rent somewhere or live in a caravan while your home is being built then you are going to have to put your furniture somewhere. If, like Rob and Alida, you're fortunate enough to have obliging family and friends with enough space to give house room to a few of your things, that's great. Otherwise, you'll be paying out for storage costs too.

You may want to allow a certain sum for landscaping. Although you probably feel that your first priority at this stage should be the house, imagine how soul-destroying it could be to end up living in a palace surrounded by the remnants of a building site. There are plenty of landscaping services that will almost certainly give you a free quote. And while outside the house, make allowances for any extra building work, such as for a garage or tool shed, that may not have been included in the initial quote for the house.

It's also worth considering how much is going to be added to your bill by those endless phone calls and faxes,

Below: Denys and Marjorie had their toolshed built with the same construction method as their house. As it was finished first, it provided a secure place to store valuable machinery or tools while the house was being completed.

Above: Changing your mind costs money. Raising the level of Denys and Marjorie's terrace higher than in the original design meant more work and therefore added expenditure.

if you're the one chasing up sub-contractors, deliveries, and so on. If you're living a long way from the site, then imagine how much extra you'll be paying out on travel. Train fares between Birmingham and Cornwall are not cheap!

Last, but definitely not least, is a contingency sum. Building can be a tricky business, which can hurl all sorts of additional unforeseen expenses at you. You can be sure that the final cost will go over even the most generous estimate. If you've employed a soil engineer to test your ground for the foundations, then you shouldn't be surprised by what happens when the trenches are dug, but frequently the building inspector will insist on some change to your plans because of unpredicted ground conditions. It's wise to put aside at least as much as ten per cent of the total budgeted cost in case the unexpected occurs. You can be ninety-nine per cent certain that it'll disappear into the black hole of your build, but if you're lucky and it doesn't, you can always put it towards that state-of-the-art dream kitchen, light fittings or even some paintings to cover the blank walls.

Building Costs

Now we really are entering the great unknown. It's impossible to be absolutely accurate when predicting how much you will spend on the building itself, but it is at least possible to be realistic. Having decided on the size of your home, you could try to work out how much it will cost per square foot. It's hard to arrive at an average cost since so much is dictated by ground conditions and site requirements, but if a main contractor quoted £60 per square foot, it wouldn't be unreasonable. For example, Carpenter, Oak & Woodland Co., the specialist company that built Denys and Marjorie's new home, quoted £70 per square foot. If you're buying from a package company, as Tim and Julia did, you have the advantage of knowing exactly what it will cost, although you should still check carefully exactly what the quote covers.

The cost of the materials naturally depends on knowing how much of everything you're going to need. A builders' merchant should be able to quote for this after studying your drawings, but it would be better to provide them with a written specification as well. A possible disadvantage to this is that the company will probably expect you to order everything from them as a result of this, when you may be planning to use different sources to get exactly the materials you want.

Perhaps it would be more satisfactory to use an independent quantity surveyor, who will be quite unbiased in their estimates. Once you have an estimate, you can decide whether or not you want to cut back on any of the detail before sending out the drawings to tender with several main contractors.

If you originate the work yourself you will make cost savings in management time, but this must be offset against your own loss of earnings. Sarah Wigglesworth and Jeremy Till found that the quantity surveyors that they decided to use came up with prices that were far in excess of what they were quoted when separate areas of the build were quoted for by specialist firms. 'We did get the quantity surveyor to price this at a fairly early stage and their price came in at roughly double what we are spending,

Below: Tim and Julia opted to buy expensive reclaimed Tudor bricks which they used for the chimney breast and the exterior of the house.

perhaps because they're not used to this type of construction.' In the end Sarah and Jeremy hired a freelance project manager who, by approaching specialist sub-contractors for different aspects of the build, brought the price right down to a manageable level. Generally speaking, quantity surveyors are more used to pricing for a conventionally run building project, such as Denys and Marjorie's, where an architect and a main contractor were employed.

Getting the Funding

Now that you've worked out the approximate total cost of your build, you can approach a likely lender. Many of the high street banks and building societies run mortgage schemes especially geared to the self-builder, or you may prefer to approach one of the specialist companies, as Sarah and Jeremy had to in the end: 'There are two parts of the project – the office and the house. Ultimately, the high street banks weren't interested at all because of the unconventional construction. We had money with the Ecology Building Society and they agreed to give us a pretty good rate on a mortgage on the office. It was better for us to finance the project by getting a loan on the office because we could offset our VAT and tax against it, whereas our capital would go on building the house.' Worried that they might not sell their house by the time their capital ran out, they also arranged a backstop with the Triodos Bank, which agreed to provide a bridging loan if that dodgy moment arose.

To be eligible for a loan, you'll need an income and some form of assets (probably your house), or you'll need to be extremely persuasive! These days no one will lend you 100 per cent of the cost. Several of the high street banks and building societies don't loan towards land purchase, while others may lend between fifty and eighty per cent of its value or of the purchase price, whichever is the lower figure. They will probably want your project to have at least outline planning permission. However, you will certainly find it easier to negotiate a mortgage to cover between seventy-five and ninety-five per cent of the building works. Unlike a conventional mortgage, the money is generally released in up to six stages, which are paid retrospectively at certain points of the build. These are: foundations to damp-proof course level, first-floor joist level, wallplate level (i.e. completion of outside wall) roofed in, plastered out and completion.

At each stage a valuer will be sent to check the work has been satisfactorily completed before the money is released. This means that you will need to make sure that you have enough to pay for everything before the first cheque arrives, unless your powers of persuasion can convince the builder to agree to a credit arrangement. You will find that every lender has different criteria attached to the mortgage, so investigate these thoroughly beforehand.

Package companies tend to sell their houses on costs per square foot. Be careful to read the brochures thoroughly, checking everything they include in that price, so that you are comparing like with like. These companies usually want the total sum paid on signature, their argument being that they have to custom-make the house in their workshops and cannot risk your reneging on the deal. But naturally, the building societies are less than keen on this idea. The way round it is to have an agreement with your solicitor whereby you lodge the money with them and they guarantee to hand it over when your house is delivered. Bear in mind though that many building societies prefer to pay the first part of the loan when the frame is erected.

Reducing Costs

What if your estimates come in too high? Is there any way you can bring them down? Here are some suggestions.

• Look at your specifications and decide whether they are too extravagant. On the other hand, if you're going to live in the house for a number of years, then you may consider it worth paying over the odds for that sauna. Don't bet that you'll get your money back when you sell, though – your dream home may not be the same as your purchaser's. But it may be advantageous to cut down on the odd feature that's not strictly necessary. Originally, Andrew and Deborah had a corridor running beside the banked wall of the water tower extension: 'But we decided it was a £1,000

Below: Because they had run out of money, Tim and Julia decided on uPVC frames rather than wood. It is an economy they now regret.

cupboard, so we cut it out as well as replacing an internal wall with a couple of pillars – that sort of thing cuts it back.'

• Do some of the work yourself. Andrew and Deborah decided to do the painting and decorating themselves, as well as the plumbing and tiling. Tim and Julia dug the service trenches on their plot. Alternatively, like Rob Roy or the Hedgehog Housing Co-op, you may choose to do almost all of it. But it is true to say that the speedier the build, the more cost-effective it is, and the easier it is on the cash flow, so think carefully about the effects of your decision.

• Live on the site – if you've got the stamina.

• Scale down the size of your house. Both Sarah and Jeremy and Michael Hird and Lindsay Harwood decided that, rather than compromise their standards, they would just make the house proportionally smaller, thereby using less materials. And, of course, Michael and Lindsey forfeited their swimming pool.

When You Can't Get the Funding

It is quite possible that all this is completely immaterial, since you may have no assets to start with and are therefore in no position to apply for a mortgage. Is self-build strictly for those with a large bank balance and a regular income? Not at all. So what on earth can you do?

With the same enthusiasm, determination, resilience and time as Paul Crouch and the other members of the Hedgehog Housing Co-op, it might be possible to join or initiate a building co-operative of your own. Paul and his partner Jennie already knew they wanted to give up their life on the road when they noticed houses being built by Diggers Self-Build, another successful co-operative scheme in Hollingbury on the edge of Brighton. They got to know someone building there. 'If you're technically homeless then it's pretty difficult to do something about your housing situation. We were advised to start our own group, but were told that it might take eight to ten years to come to fruition! Then the more we found out about other people's mistakes, the more we realized we could probably do it quicker, both in terms of getting a full participation from the Co-op and getting a bid accepted by the Housing Corporation.'

First, they had to find a housing association that wanted to work with them. Fortunately, South London Family Housing Association, which had previously supported Diggers, decided to support them. 'We were allocated an evangelical visionary figure, José Ospina, as our development worker. He devised the whole method, whereby housing associations get a grant from the government to enable the tenants to build and then rent houses. Without him, this wouldn't have happened.'

They then had to convince the council that the project would be a good, effective use of the land and that the biggest number of people possible from the council's housing waiting lists would be involved. 'We were told to keep the group very small until we'd got funding, so intially, it was myself, Jennie and two other people. This way we could offer the council seventy per cent nomination rights. They became very keen on the idea because they'd been dying to get rid of the land for the last forty years.'

That year the Co-op submitted a bid to the Housing Corporation (a government quango that allocates funds to housing associations in order to build houses) for funding and were turned down without a reason. By the following year, they'd expanded their proposals to include ideas that were sensible for ten families, who would have been through the shared experience of building their homes. They included such things as future employment, green issues and poverty reduction schemes including built-in ecological features that would save money, a credit union and a health food co-op. 'We backed it up with a lot of figures and the council were impressed. I think they must have put us at the top of the schemes they wanted funding for, so the second year we applied we got the nod – that is unheard of.'

On approval of the scheme, they immediately started asking for applications through the council's housing list. 'We ended up with the names of people who were in similar housing need, which was the only criteria we could come up with and I'm ashamed to say it, but we picked names out of a hat.' Although they lost six of the original participants – 'all of them brave enough to realize they couldn't fulfil their commitments' – the places were quickly taken up again and work began.

So, whatever your means, self-building is a real possibility as a way of realizing your dream home. Though crucial to the build, money isn't the only thing that matters: enterprise and determination have a strong hand to play too. However you solve the frequently knotty problems of finance, once achieved then you're ready to start turning your plans into long-awaited reality.

Above: Work is never completely finished on a house. When the builders leave there will inevitably be little jobs to finish off, such as the cleaning that is now required around Denys and Marjorie's windows.

Making it Happen

7

I t's all very well getting over-excited about the house that you're going to have built, but have you thought about who's actually going to take charge of getting it done? The definition of a self-builder is a very loose one and covers those who initiate the process but hand over the administration of the project to an architect and the professionals, as well as those who get down to most of the work themselves. Whichever one you decide to be, someone has to take responsibility for the site, for making sure that the right materials are to hand and in the right place, at the right time. They need to ensure that the sub-contractors are there on the right days and that everyone gets paid on time. Is that person going to be you? It could be, but if you don't want that degree of involvement in the actual construction, or if you can't afford the time, then before taking the load on your own shoulders, let's have a look at where else you could transfer it.

Letting Your Architect Take the Load

The first, perhaps most common, choice, and certainly the most expensive one, is your architect. Normally, the main contractor takes over most of the project management from the architect. However, you could come to an additional agreement with your architect whereby they organize the entire project. As they are already completely familiar with your plans and how you want the finished house to be, they will immediately know how to respond to any hitch in the proceedings, and when to refer back to you for a decision.

Once the architect has submitted the detailed plans for planning permission and building regulations approval, they will also prepare clear written

Opposite: The frame of Denys and Marjorie's atrium is assembled.

specifications and then put the job out to tender with around three main contractors or builders. When they receive the quotations, they will discuss them with you and then proceed to contract with the builder you choose, including any modifications that you may have decided on. Now work can begin and the major headaches of its organization are all theirs. Of course, that doesn't mean that you won't need to visit the site as regularly as possible to check how things are going, but it won't be you who's desperately trying to organize a late delivery or to find a missing sub-contractor.

Denys and Marjorie Randolph preferred to leave the project management to their architect, Roderick James, and his colleague Laurence Burrell, one of several architects who work with him throughout the country. Laurence was on hand to regularly oversee the build and either he or Roderick discussed particular issues with Denys and Marjorie. Roderick highly values working with a builder that he already knows: 'If you're working with a builder you know and trust, then project management isn't a problem because there's a continual dialogue with the builder. It's also important to remember that the builder will want to do it properly – he won't deliberately make the roof leak!'

However, as well as regularly visiting the site themselves, Denys and Marjorie moved into a caravan on site for three weeks during the summer of 1998 and they found their continual presence was definitely worth while at that time: 'For instance, it was particularly useful to be able to go through everything with the electrician who was there during those weeks. Because it's such a lovely house with beams everywhere, we didn't want any wires showing, so it all had to be very carefully planned.'

Because they lived so far from their Cornish chapel, Jane Fitzsimons and Gavin Allen specifically chose a local architect who would manage the project for them. This was also because they were anxious to use local craftsmen where possible. 'It probably cost us a bit more on management, but at least we weren't paranoid about it the whole time. We've always visited Gavin's dad once a month anyway, so we just came down a bit more often. It was only a three-hour journey.'

Instead of working with just one contractor, which some architects prefer, David Sheppard chose to use separate sub-contractors for each area: 'I went out into the market on each aspect of the building, trying to be extremely competitive with the tenders. I have the contacts down here so, for example, I would go to four demolition guys for prices, defining the scope of the works and finally agreeing a price with one of them. The great thing is that rather than having one main contractor, you can get a very competitive price for each part that way, and that's the way we're going to keep the budget down. The burden is making sure that everyone comes to the site on time and that there are no snags.'

Working with One Main Contractor

It may suit you better to contract directly with a main contractor, thus cutting out the additional expense of the architect's fee. If you do this, then you must be just as careful in choosing them as you have been in selecting your architect. Some of the same criteria apply.

- Go by personal recommendation if you can. Perhaps your architect will be able to advise you.
- Look at some of their recent work and talk to recent clients.
- Interview and discuss your plans with three or four potential builders and get quotes in, one of which you will have to negotiate. If you haven't specified everything initially, then there will be some notional prices included for such things as the kitchen fittings or the bathroom suite. This can sometimes be a bone of contention later on when the final accounts come in appropriately adjusted, depending on the items you've chosen, so make sure you know whether your builder is quoting the list price or the trade price.
- Use a contract that clearly sets out the terms of your agreement, then if something goes horribly wrong, you have still got something to refer back to.
- Do not allow yourself to be bulldozed into agreeing to things that you are not sure about or don't really want. If you are encouraged to use a builder's contract rather than one that you've drawn up yourself, it might be prudent to discuss it with your solicitor first before signing anything.
- Things you should be careful to include in any contract are start and finish dates, what happens if you change your mind and want something done differently (extra costs should be agreed in writing), when payments are to be made and what monies should be held back as a retention for an agreed time so that any defects can be corrected.
- Your detailed plans and written specification should be attached to the contract and referred to, defining materials, etc.
- Include a penalty clause for late completion of the whole project, or it's separate stages.

Left: Tim and Julia's driveway under construction.

• And, in case the worst comes to the worst, the contract should cover what happens if the contractor dies or disappears.

Hiring a Project Manager

If, as a self-builder, you want more involvement, or if you are an architect and don't want the full burden of the administration on your shoulders, you could follow Sarah Wigglesworth and Jeremy Till's example and hire a project manager: 'He's acting as a quantity surveyor and a contractor in one. He's organizing all the management of the project, while he brings a builder in tow, who does all the

Opposite: Great views from the scaffold at Newhaven. Always make sure your scaffolding is put up by a professional.

building. He will price the job as if he were going to build it, knowing how his builders do things, and knowing what the costs of doing things are. Because of his experience with unusual buildings, he's not phased by ours. He has a core team of people on site doing general building work and he will also manage the other sub-contractors. There's also a site agent on site all the time administering the contract, taking charge of the works and in constant contact with the project manager.'

Professional project managers have a wealth of experience on their side. They will have all the necessary contacts and organizational skills that you may be lacking but, unlike working with a builder, you can be more hands-on, agreeing in advance with your project manager which aspects of the build you're responsible for. This could include checking of deliveries, payment for materials or some of the labour. It's up to you to agree your involvement with your project manager.

Whoever you decide to work with, it's important to be clear about fees, the way in which they're calculated and how they're paid, from the start. Is the fee a fixed price or a percentage of the total building cost? If it is to be paid in instalments, when will these be scheduled in? Or will the payment be at the end of construction?

When a Project Manager is Provided

Some packagers of kit homes can provide a project manager to organize the build for you. Of course you don't have a say in who is sent, so it's just pot luck whether or not you get along with them and, indeed, whether they're an asset to your build. Generally speaking, there's no reason to assume that there should be any problems, but you could be unlucky.

Tim Cox and Julia Brock found it helped them reach their deadline when they got involved themselves. 'We found Penfolds, who dug the foundations and poured the concrete; we did the demolition ourselves and dug the service trenches, we found a chippie and people to do the second fix. The package company did organize the frame, which came with twelve carpenters, who put it up so quickly we thought we'd be well ahead of schedule. But everything ground to a halt after that. From then on, it was a continual harassment to force them to tell us who was doing the windows.'

Be Your Own Project Manager?

Finally, there is always the possibility of running the whole show yourself. But to do this, you must find almost unlimited time, patience and determination. Don't be dismissive about what you will be taking on, but equally don't underestimate the enormous sense of achievement when the job's over. If you're someone who can't organize the most simple job, then admit it and hand this one over to the professionals immediately. Don't kid yourself. Organizing a build and getting it done is a feat of near military precision and messing it up will almost certainly be extremely expensive to sort out. As David Sheppard says, of a first-time self-builder managing the project himself: 'If he's borrowing money or has a limited amount of time in which to get into the building, then I wouldn't recommend it because you can lose a lot. He would have to have a grand plan to start with, where everything is worked out to the nth degree, meaning that he knows exactly what he wants to do. But that means there won't be any room for flexibility, which I believe is key to the design and what you can do.'

Still certain that this is what you want to do? Then the most sensible way to start is by targeting key stages of the building process and making a very detailed list of these, together with the materials that each one will involve. By this time you will no doubt, like Rob, be extremely well versed, theoretically at least, in all the details involved, thanks to the available books on the subject. You will have discussed the project with your architect (who has professional knowledge and practical experience) and should have talked to suppliers and your friendly local builders' merchant, in order to get an idea of how they operate and what they would expect from an established builder. As Rob found, 'This meant that systems for things like security, safety, paying the workers, ordering materials, scheduling deliveries, insurance, filing, dealing with bad weather, VAT, bookkeeping and controlling the finances were derived in light of my own experience and knowledge, and the views that I had gleaned from others.'

Scheduling the Work

At its simplest, your list of stages and materials would run something like this:

- site clearance
- access
- foundations
- erection of shell
- roof
- insulation
- exterior cladding

- carpentry (floor joists, timber partitions)
- first fix plumbing and electricity (running the pipes and wires)
- joinery (stairs, doors, windows, cupboards)
- plastering/drylining
- second fix plumbing and electricity (fixing bathroom and kitchen fittings, connecting lighting fittings and boxes to the wires)
- finishes – decorating, tiling, flooring, etc.
- external works
- formal completion
- VAT

There are several manuals available, which contain draft schedules to help you and will guide you through the more advanced stages. The snag about these schedules is that practicalities and the need for flexibility make them constantly evolve, as Rob discovered: 'So many aspects take longer than intended, because of suppliers, for instance, that I could not rigidly impose any timetable. Things outside my control, such as weather, red tape, workload of engineers and architects, have also changed the pattern of events for me. Having meaningful budgets and budgetary control is perhaps more important than strict timetables.'

The other thing to remember is that, if you have second thoughts about it all and begin to doubt your competence, there are plenty of people from whom you can seek advice and who won't let you make any real howlers. The building inspector and valuers are going to be regular visitors and will quickly put you right if you've initiated something unsafe, and it's quite possible that the building inspector will be able to advise you about anything that you're unsure of.

Hiring Sub-contractors

Then, the major question: where are you going to get your workers (or sub-contractors) from? Unless you've already built something before, it's unlikely that they'll be crowding the pages of your address book! Rob was fortunate in having five friends with skills to bring to the project: a boat builder, two cabinetmakers, a joiner and a consultant on water-saving systems: 'We all got on really well. We convened at 8 a.m. and started the day with a ten-minute meditation in the site hut. We also shared our meal and tea breaks. We automatically broke down an efficient division of labour across jobs and all contributed a wealth of wisdom to the build.' When it came to the really specialized jobs that others could do quickly and therefore more economically, such as plastering and roofing, he hired sub-contractors. Once again, if anyone you know has employed builders in some capacity, not even necessarily in building their own home, personal recommendation is the best way to find someone. Your architect or even a friendly building inspector may be able to tip you off unofficially.

Once you've found one skilled and trustworthy sub-contractor they'll almost certainly be able to put you in touch with others, with whom they regularly work. David Sheppard has a welcome piece of advice: 'I met the guy for the demolition contract in the pub one lunchtime, 200 yards up the road from Chilsworthy chapel. If you want to be a self-builder, go to your local pub and you'll find everybody you need – electricians, builders, plumbers, the lot. Usually you get the recommendation as well because the landlord will know who's been pleased with whose work. So it's all on recommendation and then you get the best job.'

Above: Expect a major clear-up after the builders have left.

If you have the time (and you need to do this without causing offence), ask if you can see some examples of sub-contractors' recent work. Just as with the other professionals you employ, this is the best way to satisfy yourself that they're the ones you want. When hiring them you need to ascertain, preferably in writing, when they can begin, how long the job will take and whether they will need to overlap with other sub-contractors. These details must go into your schedule so that you can see easily who's arriving on site, and when.

More words of advice on hiring sub-contractors from David Sheppard: 'You always come up against little problems that might delay the programme, then you have to delay someone else before that other person can finish. That's all down to co-ordination. Make sure you give enough time for each aspect of the job to take place. But then you have overlaps, which are additional complications. For example, you might have the carpenter putting up partitions, who wants the

Right: Rob Roy took his friends to Cumbria to watch a similar house being built. Then they put the theory into practice.

plumber there, putting his plumbing in, before a plasterer plasters the walls. Getting all that right is something you get with experience. You know when a building's at a certain stage to get someone else in to do another part of the work.'

Agreeing Prices and Organizing Materials

You will also have to negotiate a price, either fixed for the whole job or on a daily rate, and at which stages it is to be paid. Be specific about what it is you are asking your sub-contractors to do. It's also important to be clear about who you are employing for labour only and who will 'supply and fix', i.e. bring the necessary materials with them. Nothing could be more annoying than having the plasterer arrive on the due day, but finding that neither of you have bought the plaster, each thinking the other one was responsible for its supply – and it could cost another day's delay.

Talking of materials: where are they coming from? By this time you'll know what you want and it will be a question of locating them. A local builders' merchant is the obvious first port of call. Check out the ones near you and compare their prices. You need to open a trade account so that you're eligible for trade discounts. It's possible that the more you buy in one place, the better the discounts will be. However, you may prefer to shop around for separate items. Consider carefully: what you may save in money you could spend in the initial legwork and phone calls needed to find the materials. It does, however, almost certainly give you a wider choice of materials.

Next to consider is when you want the materials and where you're going to store them once you've got them. Obviously, you don't want expensive materials lying about for weeks, getting damaged by the weather or tempting thieves. It's important to get the deliveries timed as closely as possible to the date that the materials are going to be used. The character of the site is going to be an important consideration too. What sort of space do you have available? How close will the delivery lorries be able to get to the building? If there's a long drive with no space at the end of it, make sure that the materials to be used first are nearest to the house.

Keeping Records

Some people suggest that you should keep a diary of the build. This is both fun to look back on and also a useful asset when arguing over a delivery date or the length of time that a particular sub-contractor has been on site. It's also vital to keep a record of every bill paid. Self-builders are not liable for VAT and can make a once-only claim for a refund from the VAT office within three months of having completed construction. If you file everything away carefully, it will save you a lot of trouble later on. Your claim should cover: 'all ordinarily incorporated building materials'. If you're not clear what that means, look at VAT Notice 719 which is available from HM Customs and Excise.

Avoiding Pitfalls

But back to the site. In your new role as project manager it's your responsibility to ensure you have adequate insurance (see Chapter 6, Money Matters, pages 110–123), that the site is tidy and safe, and that the security is as thorough as you can make it. Every evening you will have to check that everything has been properly cleared up and chucked into the skips that you will have ordered in advance and arranged to be replaced when full. You will also need to order the scaffolding. It is not recommended that you skimp on costs and erect the scaffolding yourself: too many lives are at risk. This is one instance when the experts definitely do know best. Besides, they'll have it up far quicker than you and a few mates ever could, so don't even think about it. There's going to be some valuable machinery left on site overnight, not to mention unused materials, so if you can't lock it all up, it might be necessary to invest in some sort of fencing that will keep all but the most determined thieves or vandals out.

What are the pitfalls that you are most likely to encounter? Perhaps the most obvious and the most frustrating ones are the non-delivery of materials and subsequent disappearance of your sub-contractors to another site. To keep on top

Overleaf: Local builders at work on the Chilsworthy chapel.

of the construction, you've got to be ahead of the game. The only way you can be sure the materials are going to be in the right place at the right time is by ordering them early. It ought to be simple enough to find out delivery times, whether it is for a bag of cement or a quantity of specially chosen roof tiles. So find out well before the building is due to start and make allowances for them.

Another crucial thing to remember is not to under-order. Either your quantity surveyor or your builders' merchant should have advised you on the right amounts of materials after looking at your plans and written specifications, but it's wise to add on an extra five per cent in case of breakages or miscalculation. Otherwise you may find yourself in Tim and Julia's position on Easter Saturday, when the builder's sand ran out. 'Rather than see them go away we went and bought sand by the bag load from B&Q, similarly cement. You just fill the gaps or they'll walk off site and you have to chase them until they come back a fortnight later. We made countless trips to keep them going.'

When the materials arrive, make sure you check them against the order and the delivery note as mistakes can happen. Most suppliers will eventually take back the surplus stock if you've kept it in good condition.

Another potential problem can be in checking the work. It's essential that you visit the site every day to make sure that the plans are being carried out properly and that the work's being carried out to a sufficiently high standard. In translating the drawing into reality, it's always possible to slightly misinterpret the original, so it's worth making absolutely certain that it's as you and your architect intended. Similarly, the original design, while perfect on paper, may for some reason need to be slightly altered to accommodate something else and you'll want to be able to discuss the implications of any change with the sub-contractor. Again, communication is everything. And being there is everything else, making sure the work is happening. Julia advises, 'Be there with a bag of doughnuts all the time. Tim bribed them with about 60,000 doughnuts from Somerfields over the course of three weeks.'

Success Stories

Apart from superb organization, the only sure way of avoiding the pitfalls is through experience. And if you're not a professional? Deborah Mills intended to project-manage the conversion of the Coleshill water tower, but only after the extension was complete and they would be able to live on site: 'The new extension was down to one contractor because we needed that to go up as soon as possible.

Left: Each piece of wood arrived individually marked at Denys and Marjorie's site so it was clear to see how they fitted together.

But I went there on a daily basis and picked up tips on how to do things, and how to do them differently. It's all down to communication. I gave everybody as much information as I possibly could, even things I didn't really want them to know!'

Can you do it yourself?

Perhaps, like Rob or the Hedgehog Housing Co-op, you may want to, or have to, become more involved still. Besides managing the build how much can you physically do yourself? The answer is simple: it's up to you.

Denys and Marjorie left things entirely to the experts. Tim and Julia, however, tried their hand at digging: 'You need some sort of mechanical digger to dig the trenches, so the best thing to do is to hire a man who can do it better than you. We hired a machine for a day but after an hour it was a nightmare. We dug the trenches

Above: Project managing by principle – the Hedgehog Housing Co-op's members made a pact that all the houses would be completed together, so that everyone could move in at the same time.

for the gas, electricity and water, and we laid the pipes in those and in through the house, which saved us a lot of money. We thought it would be complicated getting the services from the road to the house, but the companies were very helpful and in the end we had one trench with all the different ductings in it.'

Rob felt strongly that he wanted to run the build: 'I work best when I'm on my own or when I'm running a team.' Having done that, he has a number of useful tips for the novice:

• Be obsessed about the project and how it should all fit together. Think everything through so you know what action you or others should take, and when.

• Do not be afraid to ask professionals what they think. This includes builders, planning officers, building control inspectors, architects, builders' merchants, suppliers' technical helplines and so on.

• Keep the site and your office as tidy and ordered as possible.

• Make sure your sub-contractors know you are boss.

Of course, it's the nature of the deal that means that Paul Crouch and his fellow members of the Hedgehog Housing Co-op are building the houses themselves. Each household is committed to putting thirty hours of labour into the project every week. One of the Co-op members, who had no previous experience of building, claims: 'Like most things, it's over-rated. Once you've got the basic principles, it's just practice.' Whereas Paul, a welder, had never worked with wood and simply says: 'I was told I would be able to build by someone I believed.' As far as he is concerned, the option of building following the principles of the Walter Segal method is something that anyone can do, provided they don't underestimate the time and effort involved. However, the Co-op has used sub-contractors in certain areas, such as the plumbing and heating (where possible, using the self-builders as labourers) or, in the case of the roofing or insulation, where the suppliers insist they fix the product themselves otherwise they won't give a guarantee. The Hedgehog Housing Co-op also employed a site manager, who

Overleaf: Denys and Marjorie's roof goes on.

Below: Women builders are not a common sight except in Brighton at the Hedgehog Housing Co-op.

came to the site three days a week. Geoff Stow works for the Walter Segal Trust as well. His is a rather exceptional role because while performing the usual role of overseeing the activities on site, getting the materials on site and finding the sub-contractors, he is also the person responsible for devising training programmes in certain areas (e.g. carpentry, first aid, health and safety) and getting the site set up in the first place, including toilets, canteen, storage facilities and a crêche. Constructing these gave the group a chance to work together and use certain tools first before they went straight into the business of building their houses. Most important of all though is his role in keeping the group together: 'If you lose the group, the whole thing dies. You've got to maintain a good atmosphere because they're all going to be living there afterwards.' Lastly, he acts as the focus – the person everyone (sub-contractors, builders, architect, etc.) can turn to when there's a problem.

Geoff's advice echoes that of David Sheppard: 'You should work out how long it's going to take and double it! The little details can take forever. The main problem is linking your pace with delivery of materials. A lot of it is being organized enough to know what the next thing you want is, having found a supplier and got a price, at the same time arranging deliveries at the time you will need them.'

It's true that the standard of a self-built home tends to be higher than that built by a contractor for the simple reason that self-builders aren't experienced enough to know what they can get away with, so they don't take short-cuts. And of course, they know who's going to be living there and who is likely to suffer from any sloppy work afterwards.

Choosing Your Role

Which stance should you adopt as a self-builder – take a step back and leave it to the professionals, or roll up your sleeves and do it, or as much of it as you can, yourself? Before you decide, weigh up how much time you have because it will almost certainly take longer if you're in the driving seat yourself, rather than someone with experience on their side. You must also decide what you can afford to do. It can be a full-time occupation, and during that time, unless you are like Rob and can busy yourself with freelance activities such as his tax consultancy or log rack company, what will you be living off? Whichever path you choose, there's no doubt that the satisfaction and pride that you will experience in achieving your dream home yourself will be overwhelming.

How Green

8

can You Go?

We are slowly but surely destroying the planet. Warnings about the depletion of the world's resources and global warming make the headlines almost every day. In an increasingly ecology-conscious world, isn't it down to us to do whatever we can to combat these threats? In 1992 the Rio Earth Summit brought the situation to the world's attention. Local Agenda 21 was agreed by all the nations present and stresses the need to avoid environmental catastrophe without impeding a steady improvement in the quality of life. It provides a framework for working towards meeting people's needs through the use of local resources without depleting them or exploiting the resources belonging to other countries.

Whatever has this got to do with your dream home? The answer is: everything. It is almost certain that the greenhouse effect is caused by the relentless increase in the amount of carbon dioxide released into the atmosphere by our burning more and more fossil fuels. In an advanced economy, people consume enormous amounts of energy in their day-to-day lives, and a third of the carbon dioxide released through energy consumption in this country comes from private households. Energy is used to manufacture every part of a building. Ten per cent of the world's carbon dioxide emissions is produced by the construction industry. More energy goes into transporting the materials to the site and putting them in place. Together, these factors create the 'embodied energy' of a product. You should consider the following:

• Ask yourself how much impact a manufacturing process or method of transport has on the environment.

• Question whether the expense of energy can be 'paid back', for example by using more energy-efficient materials.

• If it cannot be paid back, consider whether more natural materials, which use less energy in their production, could be used instead.

• Are there alternative sources of power that you can use without significant discomfort? If everyone began to regard fossil fuels purely as a back-up, rather than as a primary source of energy, we would be a good deal nearer to solving environmental problems.

• As well as saving energy, you should also consider how much recycling you can do and which materials you can use from renewable resources.

• Finally, you should think about toxicity. Until relatively recently asbestos was used routinely and on a huge scale in construction, being prized for its fire-resistant properties. How many of today's innovative building materials carry a similar hidden health risk? For example, MDF (medium-density fibreboard) has a high formaldehyde content that is slowly released over the years. Formaldehyde is one of various noxious volatile organic compounds (VOCs) that are routinely present in different building products. Others are organochlorines, which are found in a wide range of plastic products, including PVC and synthetic paints. Timber preservatives, used so readily these days, contain extremely toxic chemicals that can affect the person applying them and which also leech into the atmosphere for some time after application.

What Can You Do?

The extent to which you can address these questions in building your home depends on your own personal level of commitment. Currently, one of the most extreme eco-building movements is being developed in German-speaking countries, where *Baubiologie* (building biology) defines the house as your third skin (clothes being your second). Just as you wouldn't dress either for health or for comfort entirely in plastic or rubber, nor should you live in a building that is completely sealed, thanks to the use of impermeable materials.

For over a century we have been constructing buildings using Portland cement and gypsum plaster, neither of which transpire gas and water molecules. More recently, the introduction of high-performance synthetic paints, such as acrylics and vinyl emulsions, has meant that we now coat the inside of our buildings with layers of plastic that cannot transpire, preventing moisture that is naturally present

Right: The Hedgehog Housing Co-op are not just building their homes, they are building a community. One of the ideals of this is being friendly to the planet.

in the walls to freely pass from it. *Baubiologie* uses traditional materials, such as wood, clay, lime mortar and earth. These all 'breathe' by enabling air and moisture to move through them without cooling the house but improving the atmosphere inside, regulating humidity and reducing the likelihood of rising damp.

The idea is that balance and harmony should exist between buildings, people and nature. These homes, so the theory goes, are not only built to benefit the planet, but also to be health-giving for the minds and spirits of the people who will be living in them.

Housing Projects to Protect the Environment

During the 1980s and 1990s many research projects have been set up to develop housing ideas that can protect the planet through their use of alternative energy sources and recycling systems. Prototypes have been built, such as the Eco Home in Los Angeles and the Eco House in Bristol. In Wales, the Centre for Alternative Technology, founded in the 1970s in a derelict slate quarry, is a living demonstration of how new technologies can provide ecological solutions to the world's problems.

Initiatives and experiments in eco-living are happening all around us, often on a tiny scale and far from the public eye. In 1962 a small community was founded near Findhorn in Scotland. Since 1989 they have built a 'planetary' (or 'ecological') village, that aims to be spiritually, economically, ecologically and culturally sustainable along the lines of *Baubiologie*. They were anxious that the houses should harmonize with the landscape, sharing as many amenities as possible and be 'absolutely state-of-the-art "green", employing the best methods and materials throughout in terms of energy, the environment and health considerations.' A similar anonymous community in the Pembroke National Park in Wales was recently discovered when a pilot flying overhead spotted their solar panels glinting in the sun.

Small but dedicated enterprises, like the ones described above, exist all over the world, where people have decided to create their own natural environments by building along strict ecological principles and then adapting themselves to new sustainable ways of life, growing their own food, and using local materials and renewable sources of power. These projects often get their inspiration from age-old ideals about self-sufficiency and the 'simple life'. From one point of view they confront advanced capitalism with a devastating critique; from another, they are simply impractical pipedreams.

Eco-ideas

But you don't have to join an alternative community to contribute to either your own or the planet's well-being. People have developed plenty of alternative solutions for the concerned individual. Some of the most radical are still at the drawing board stage. The Forest House, designed by Steve Johnson as a prototype for future living, may appeal to

Below: Sarah and Jeremy drew up an eco-plan of their house and office confirming all the eco-friendly features they wanted to include. (*For information only, not for construction.*)

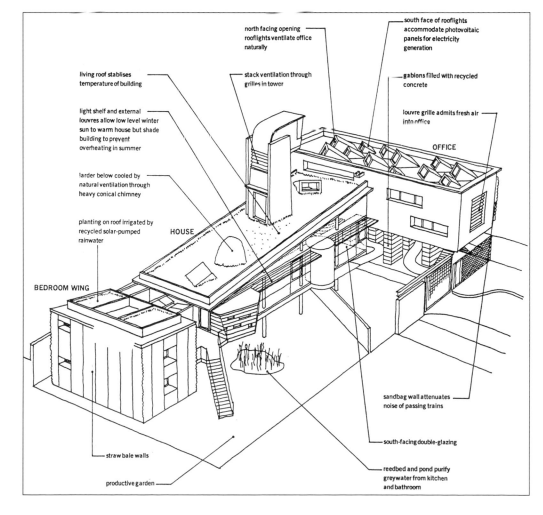

you. It is intended to be wholly self-sufficient and built way up in the treetops, where it could not affect the ecosystems below it.

Alternatively, you could snuggle up in one of Roger Dean's curvilinear 'Dean' houses, which nestle into the ground, are ecologically sound, yet designed for comfort with their rounded womb-like rooms. Or can you imagine living in a house made from discarded tyres and aluminium cans? These are the 'earthships' in New Mexico that offer yet another approach to sustainable living. Constructed from old tyres, rammed with earth to make them hard as bricks, and with inner walls of cans and cement, these can be built anywhere and run very cheaply. With their solar panels and wind generators, they do not need conventional externally powered heating systems. They are extremely efficient in water use, catching, storing and recycling all water with minimum wastage. Their website proclaims: 'Earthships are a new approach to living that involves interfacing with the earth – peacefully co-existing and thriving in nature.' And then of course you could always go underground…

Taking the Middle Path

All the ideas described so far are extreme. Not everyone can muster the burning commitment to carry such projects through. Don't worry: you needn't be a fully paid-up eco-warrior to do your bit. You can incorporate all sorts of ecologically sound features in your home without necessarily compromising its design or essence in any way, and you can save yourself money too. What's more, you'll find that you don't always have to be technologically innovative about this.

When Rob Roy and Alida Saunders made the decision to build their own home, they were already interested and involved in permaculture, an ecological design system the central principle of which dictates that we should look after the earth using its systems to supply our needs without either destroying them or damaging their production abilities. Rob takes a rational middle path through the eco-debate: 'It has been polarized by loud voices at either end of the spectrum. There are those saying there's no such thing as global warming and any allowance we give to the green movement would be economic madness, while on the other hand you've got radical green fundamentalists claiming all economic growth leads to environmental degradation. Personally, I think the answer lies somewhere in the middle. We've got to use our resources in a sustainable manner, which doesn't mean we're not going to have dishwashers or washing machines, just that we're going to have very efficient ones.' In designing their eco-house, Rob looked extremely carefully into

From forest to framework, Carpenter Oak prepares Denys and Marjorie's timber frame.

every aspect of green building and ways of cutting down on energy use, while creating a viable and comfortable home for himself, Alida and their three daughters.

Structure

Timber is the material most favoured by the eco-lobby and with good reason. If grown in properly managed forests it is a sustainable material that has only used natural energy in its production, and it's extremely durable too. Timber also has a low level of embodied energy since it requires very little processing before use. It is also relatively easy to work with and, using the Walter Segal post-and-beam method, unskilled people can build with it.

Rob opted for a similar method of construction. An important factor in his decision was the fact that the frame is raised on stilts, which rest on concrete pads. These obviously use much less concrete than traditional foundations so they 'tread more lightly on the earth', making far less impact on the environment. Lifting the house off the earth also has the advantage of letting air flow around it, not forgetting that it also makes a place for chickens to scratch in and a shelter for logs to be stored. Instead of using timber beams, Rob decided to use Masonite 'I-beams', which are engineered to be strong, but use less wood in their construction than solid beams.

As we saw in Chapter 4 (Material Facts, pages 72–97) there are other traditional ways of building that are being revived today. Straw bales, earth or cob, for example, are all green materials that have low embodied energy, high insulative values and surfaces that breathe, and they are all made from wholly renewable resources. Cob and its variants, such as rammed earth, have been re-examined in the past decade or so as the starting point for earth-sheltered designs.

Alternative Energy Sources

Across the world, the sun is the most obvious natural source of energy that is freely available to us. Solar power can be harnessed by trapping the sun's heat in solar panels, converting its energy to heat your water. It's not going to give you a steaming bath in the middle of a British winter, but it will save on your bills since the more conventional ways of heating won't have to work as hard. The panels can be positioned reasonably discreetly without compromising the design of the house. For example, Rob 's panels are hidden on the verandah roof. Photovoltaic panels are also available. Unfortunately, these are still much more expensive than solar

Opposite top and below:
'Treading lightly on the earth'. Both Rob and Alida and the Hedgehog Housing Co-op had eco-friendly foundations. Firstly holes are dug, as at Suffolk, top. These are then filled with concrete in which the stilts stand, as at Brighton, below.

panels but they efficiently convert solar light to electric power.

Passive solar power relies simply on orientating your house so that it faces south and – following the example of Rob, the Hedgehog Housing Co-op, and Sarah Wigglesworth and Jeremy Till – putting your largest windows on that side of the house. The sunlight will shine into the exposed rooms, so heating them. However, that's not enough in itself. It's important to understand 'thermal mass', a concept much loved by eco-builders, which means the capacity of a substance to retain heat. The sunlight needs to fall on solid masses, such as the floor and walls, that will hold the heat and release it at night on a similar principle to a storage heater. Remember that stone and concrete retain heat better than wood. Concrete, perhaps surprisingly, finds favour with environmentalists because it has low embodied energy too. In the summer you may need blinds at the windows so that the house doesn't overheat. But they should be removed in the winter, when the sun is lower in the sky and frequently less evident! The foliage of a medium or small tree, such as an apple, planted to the south of the window provides a natural screen that disappears in the autumn.

Both water and wind offer sources of alternative power that have been used for centuries. However, the equipment needed to make them generate electricity for an individual dwelling is tremendously expensive and is out of the reach of the average self-builder. It is also less cost-effective and unless you are going for a complete life-change, you will be unlikely to go down this path, though Rob and Alida do have plans for a wind generator in the future.

Above: Photovoltaic panels are an efficient way to convert solar energy into electricity.

Handling Heat Loss

Once the house is warmed up in winter, you will want it to stay that way. This means considering how you're going to insulate it. In 1995 building regulations were changed to upgrade the standard of energy efficiency in new houses and all are now energy-rated and must meet certain levels, known as SAP ratings. It's true to say that for years most self-builders have been only too aware of the need to tighten up this aspect of their building; nearly all self-built houses easily exceed the British regulations which, incidentally, fall well below those set in other European countries. In a building there are three main ways in which heat can be lost:

- through the fabric of the walls, roof, floor, doors and windows – these elements of the house's skin will conduct heat away.
- via open windows used for ventilation.
- when carried away on draughts.

Cavity walls present a solution to the first problem. There are plenty of synthetic materials available to keep your house warm, but these are not necessarily acceptable to anyone who prioritizes ecology. Look at the natural alternatives of cork, straw, wood, fibreboard and cellulose, and consider their cost effectiveness and durability. Rob chose Warmcel, which is a cellulose fluff made from reconstituted newsprint: 'Sometimes you get a yellow batch, so I knew a few tons of *Yellow Pages* have gone in!' It's effective, non-toxic, non-irritant and non-flammable.

Similarly, the roof space should be insulated thoroughly to prevent heat escaping upwards. Layers of insulation can be put beneath the rafters in a conventional or even a turf-roofed house. Turf does provide some insulation of its own and while it isn't completely efficient, it is additionally favoured by environmentalists because it replaces the earth you've dug up for the foundations of the building, thus closing the ecological circle.

Windows are another obvious place where heat can be lost. These days the manufacture of glass has become so sophisticated that you have a choice of solutions. Denys and Marjorie Randolph used Pilkington K glass, which is chemically coated to allow the light in, but prevents heat from making its way back out. Rob opted not for double- but triple-glazing, which is more effective still. There are all sorts of variations on the market for you to choose from, including units with additional space between the layers of glazing to increase their effectiveness (this makes for better sound insulation too), or the

Below: The Hedgehog Housing Co-op's houses wait for their turf roofs.

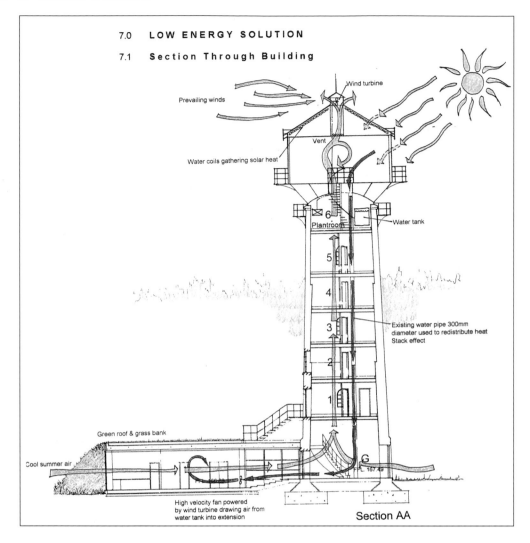

7.0 LOW ENERGY SOLUTION

7.1 Section Through Building

Wind turbine

Prevailing winds

Vent

Water coils gathering solar heat

6
Plantroom

Water tank

5

4

3

Existing water pipe 300mm
diameter used to redistribute heat
Stack effect

2

1

Green roof & grass bank

Cool summer air

G
L 167.49

High velocity fan powered
by wind turbine drawing air from
water tank into extension

Section AA

Above: Andrew ecologically exploited the industrial legacy of the water tower by using the old water pipe to transmit hot air from the top of the tower to the new extension. *(For information only, not for construction.)*

Opposite top: Underfloor heating may be expensive to install but it saves both energy and money in the long run.

Opposite below: Denys waged a determined crusade to get his heat pump installed. It may have seemed an expensive investment but he will soon be enjoying vastly reduced electricity bills as a result.

intrusion of argon, an inert gas that is commonly used between the layers of glazing, which again resists heat loss.

Draughts should be avoided by the careful construction of your home, particularly in making sure that the doors and windows fit properly. Look at the layout of the rooms, which can make a considerable difference too. Rob's house has been arranged so that rooms which don't need heating, such as the larder and drying room, are aligned along the north side of the house, providing an extra insulating barrier between the living area and the outside. The porches have the same function and double up as draught lobbies.

Heating

Central heating is such a comfort to most of us that life without it must seem like an unlikely, not to say unpleasant, proposition. But a thoroughly well-planned eco-house should have no need for central heating at all, thus saving both money and fossil-fuel reserves. Rob has been extremely careful in insulating his house, taking into account its position, calculating the balance between unavoidable heat loss and the heat that comes from the mechanical utilities, and from the people living in it. If something as apparently insignificant as a cat were to suddenly take up residence, the temperature levels of the house would be thrown out of kilter. 'Because this house is superinsulated, we don't need conventional central heating. In the depths of winter we may need a small amount of space heating and so we'll use a couple of small wood-burning stoves.' He also allowed for a system of small pipes embedded in a couple of internal walls. These contain water that is heated either by the solar panels or the wood-burning stove, turning the whole wall into a radiating element: 'It's far more efficient than a conventional central heating system and gives a more comfortable feel to the living space.'

Underfloor heating was pioneered by the Romans and is all the rage at the moment. It certainly has the advantage over conventional radiator central heating in that running costs are much lower and rooms are evenly heated. Various systems are available that all work slightly differently, so it's up to you to shop around for the one that suits you best. They can be run on electricity but Denys's pride and joy is his heat pump, which involves great lengths of pipe buried in trenches behind the house. Working rather like a fridge in reverse, it collects heat from the earth and delivers it to the house: 'Before, we've had oil-fired boilers which were endless trouble. But the running costs of this should be about a third.' So his not inconsiderable investment should have a relatively quick payback.

There is a plethora of more or less energy-efficient methods of heating your home. A visit to the self-build shows or the Building Centre in London's Store Street will swiftly initiate you into the baffling world of condensing boilers and heat recovery ventilation systems. These can be expensive at first glance, but the energy they save in the long run and the positive effect on your future bills, not forgetting the planet, may well make them a sensible option for you.

Water

Almost every summer the hosepipe bans return in force with dire warnings about the

nation's water shortage and the depletion of the water table. If you're building a house from scratch, there's a lot you can do to save water, apart from recycling as much of it as you can.

Thousands of litres of water are wasted every day in normal day-to-day household use. There are two classifications of waste water: 'grey' which comes from sinks and baths, and 'black', which is more heavily polluted and comes from toilets or sinks and dishwashers where a lot of detergent is used. Rob looked carefully into ways of reducing his family's consumption of water: 'Water's a resource which is vital to everybody. If we are to have enough to go round we must limit the demand. We need quality water for drinking and washing, but not for everything else.' He has installed a 5,000-litre (7,350 gallon) tank that will collect rainwater from the house and garage roofs and pump it to the washing machine and dishwasher, or it can be used for watering the garden. The high-quality water used in the sinks, bathroom and shower will then be collected and used to flush the toilets, which can use either 3 or 6 litres (5 ¼ or 10 ½ pints) of water, depending on the touch of a button.

Below: Barrels such as this can be used to collect rainwater for recycling.

Rob has decided that besides using a small septic tank, they will have a system of reed-beds, which will process the rest of the waste water. The reed-beds filter and treat the waste water until it is clean enough to flow into a wildlife pond at the end of the garden: 'We will still probably use 800 to 1,000 litres of water a day, but conventional households use up to 2,500 litres a day for the same sized family.' It is possible to use a more complicated system of reed-beds to deal with black water (sewage) but in practice they are trickier to manage.

Sarah Wigglesworth and Jeremy Till are using the first urban composting toilet in Britain. These don't use any water at all, they produce fertilizer for your garden and they don't smell.

Toxins

Most people are blissfully unaware of the toxic substances that go into the construction of a building. Just because something is used routinely doesn't mean that it is necessarily safe. Builders' flavour of the month at the moment is MDF, which, like particle board and plywood, contains formaldehyde (a VOC or Volatile

Organic Compound) thought to be released as a noxious vapour (see page 147). It can irritate the eyes, skin and respiratory system and the vapour may cause headaches, dizziness and nausea and is thought to be carcinogenic. It is also found in some synthetic carpets and underlays, in glues that are used to fix floor and wall tiles and in vinyl plastics.

As buildings become more tightly sealed, internal pollution becomes increasingly concentrated so you should try to avoid all potentially hazardous substances. Synthetic paints, varnishes, glues and a variety of timber treatments contain organochlorines, which are the most potent of VOCs and these can cause depression, headaches and even damage to the liver and kidneys. Phenols are found in resins and plastics, including paints and varnishes. They can burn the skin and are dangerous if inhaled. Some paints also contain traces of metals that are potentially harmful. The majority of external softwood timber is pressure treated or 'tanalized', which results in copper, chrome and arsenic being present in the wood. No data is available for the copper and chrome, but it is known that if the timber becomes wet, minute amounts of arsenic leech out of the wood's surface.

What can you do? Wherever possible, you can use alternative materials that

Above: Rob and Alida's architect, Neil Winder, has two composting toilets in this extension. In his system you use one toilet for several months before switching to the second while the first composts.

may be more expensive but have the distinct advantage of improving the atmosphere of your home. Use renewable hardwoods, untreated timbers, natural fibre carpets and traditional glues. If you have to treat the timber, borax, sodium carbonate, linseed oil and beeswax are among the safer, yet effective, options, though there are some commercial treatments that are more environmentally friendly than others. Check with the makers. Avoid plastics such as PVC wherever possible and when painting, at the very least make sure the windows are kept wide open. Preferably choose water-based paints or those from natural paint manufacturers, such as Keims. The same goes for varnishes – the natural option is always preferable. Brand names such as Auro and Nutshell are successful manufacturers in this area.

Low-level Radiation

Radon is a tasteless, odourless radioactive gas that has recently been the cause of a health scare and found to be concentrated in particular regions. This is not a general problem, but if you're proposing to live in one of the threatened areas, such as Devon, Cornwall or parts of Somerset, it's wise to have a radon test. The National Radiological Protection Board supplies test kits. The most dangerous source is the ground beneath a building, where gas can seep up into the lower floors. In Chilsworthy chapel, Jane Fitzsimons and Gavin Allen have spent an extra £1,000 on gas-proof layers and flooring so that the radon from the granite rock below flows round the building and not into it. In the internal garden, where it's obviously impossible to give it that kind of treatment, pumps running on solar power will pump it out.

Electromagnetic Fields (EMFs)

EMFs are produced when electricity is used and there is some concern as to whether exposure to them, particularly low frequency fields, is harmful. Proximity to pylons has been regarded with suspicion for some time as a possible cause of both physical and mental health problems, though there have been studies that have disproved these theories. This is an area where Rob has been particularly vigilant, having experienced its effect on one of his daughters: 'When we dramatically reduced the EMFs in her room, the aspects of her behaviour that were causing a problem changed almost overnight.' As a result, they are not using conventional domestic ring main circuits in the house but radial circuits, which should reduce the level of EMFs. They are also connecting demand switches, which prevent the AC current from sitting around when the circuit's not being used. Thirdly, they are keeping their water pipes away from the electricity cables: 'In conventional housing the builders put it all in one trench, which means that the water is constantly in a very strong electromagnetic field. It means that potentially the water is giving off EMFs.'

Recycling

Of all the ideas to have come out of the green movement, 'recycling' is the one that has most caught the public imagination. In fact, it is little more than the principle of thrift that has been practised for generations, by the ragpickers and 'mudlarks' in Dickens' London and present in the austerity measures of the post-war period.

Below: Tim and Julia used reclaimed railway sleepers to echo the tidebreaks on a beach.

With the arrival of the 'affluent society' (when material wealth was measurable in terms of the number of dustbins a household could fill), recycling was forgotten, but now it is back. This is a contribution that we can all make in our daily lives, but the self-builder has a rather unusual opportunity to re-use materials that might otherwise go into the municipal incinerator or landfill site – reclaimed floorboards, timber, tiles, bricks, dado rails, doors, window frames, fireplaces, baths and even plaster mouldings, all of which have the added attraction of being made from safe, traditional materials.

You may consider that the incorporation of all these green ideas and elements makes the planning of your home just too complicated and stressful. But spare a thought for the planet too. Even if you don't want to embark on any kind of alternative lifestyle, there are many modifications that you can still make to your home that will contribute to both your own wellbeing and to the environment. There's no need to sacrifice the quality of your home in the name of principle and being eco-friendly can be cost-effective too. As the green movement exhorts: 'Think globally, act locally'. Every little helps.

Finishing Touches

9

The shelves of book shops and libraries across the country groan with volumes dedicated to the art of interior decoration. Together with cookery and gardening, it is one of the nation's great passions so it seems both natural and desirable that this book should deal with the decorating element of building a house. After all, the great rumbling project that you have dedicated weeks and months, perhaps even years, of your time to now requires attention in this department.

Because there are so many books on the subject of decorating out there in the market already, it seems a pointless task to condense an entire worldly wealth of information into just one chapter. There is no point in sketching over the intricacies of paint techniques or making passing references to French Provincial style when these are expertly covered in other books (see Further Reading, page 192). However, what often isn't covered in those books is some of the underlying principles of how houses are best decorated, what makes decoration work well and what frame of mind you should adopt when decorating both the inside and outside of a 'virgin' house from top to bottom.

Decorating the Indoor/Outdoor Space

We already know the important principle championed by architects that a good building works well whichever way you experience it – from the inside, outside, looking down on it, in the context of the landscape in which it sits, and so on. And just as we might expect a building's architectural experiences to be related to each other (in the way that you can sometimes recognize the same building from the inside, as well as the outside), so it's not unreasonable to think of the building's decoration on the inside as relating to the colour and design on the exterior. This corresponds to the German idea of *Baubologie* that we explored in Chapter 8 (How Green Can You Go? pages 146–161), where the building is seen as a third, breathing skin; something that doesn't put up a barrier to the world but instead allows our experiences to flow freely in and out of our homes. Although this idea sounds abstract, it is easily illustrated by the way in which people are now designing their homes and gardens to relate to each other through the use of glass walls, terraces and the concept of an 'outdoor room' garden that can be used for entertaining, relaxing and play.

With just a glass wall between your sitting room and your painted, decorated garden, you can begin to see why it might be important to treat both spaces in a coherent way. This is something that minimalism does particularly well, mainly because it interests itself in the use of 'honest' materials. So, for example, slate, unvarnished wood and stone (all naturally occurring outdoor materials) find their way into the home, where they are appreciated for their raw qualities. Meanwhile, in a minimalist garden, the rectilinear sparseness of the interior of the house is often applied as the dominant aesthetic and so the two spaces are joined up.

Environments

The idea of your house being a transparent 'skin' works only up to a point. When it comes to the way in which we decorate, it might be better to think of the concept slightly differently, in terms of the word 'environment'. We live in three enveloping environments: the interiors of our homes, the built environment (whether urban or rural) and the natural environment. It's usual for each of these to have their own specialists, i.e. interior designers, architects and environmentalists. But building your

Below: Nowadays the concept of 'home' extends beyond the four walls into the surrounding garden, where other 'rooms' can be created. Keep the transition between indoor and outdoor as smooth as possible, as here in Tim and Julia's home.

own home, whether you employ any of these specialists or none at all, is an activity that allows you to manipulate and cross over the thresholds of these three environments in a very flexible way. You have control over all of them.

When it comes to the third, wider natural environment, your whole approach to the resources and the energy that you use to put up, and live in, your home has a powerful effect on how much you damage, or care for, the world. You can make environmentally friendly choices when selecting your decorating materials: opt for non-petroleum paint types, such as linseed oil, distemper, casein, silicate or limewash paints; use non-polluting woodcare products; and specify renders made from local lime rather than cement.

The wider environment apart, it is really in the other two environments, the built and the interior, that decoration really comes into its own. For example, the immediate environment is the interior of our home. In this space we have an obligation to ourselves and our families to provide a pleasant and stimulating surrounding for each person to flourish in. If you think of interior decorating as being an irrelevant add-on to a build, then think again. Decoration can be used to consolidate your family life, thus creating the environment that you both want and need from an empty box. Without it, houses can be alienating shells. It is our first environment.

Of course, the house usually sits in some kind of community and always in a type of landscape context that involves other people, whether this means passing traffic, pedestrians or even neighbours looking at your house from across a deserted valley. This is the built environment, the one that crowds in on us in Britain. Our obligation here is not to offend or taunt our neighbours with aggressive buildings, but to appeal to their better natures. Modern architecture can do this very well, as we found in the series. The arguments about whether a building should be modern or traditional, vernacular or international in style, usually only surface when a modern design is unsympathetic to the site or just badly thought out. It's interesting that

Below: Tim and Julia's blue living room reflects the colour of the sea below the house.

Sarah Wigglesworth and Jeremy Till's Islington project and Andrew Tate and Deborah Mills' water tower build were both very contemporary designs that had the full support of the local community. The real distinction, from which these arguments distract us, is the one between good and bad architecture.

Local Colour

The way in which we paint our house and the materials used to clad and render it should all reflect the obligation described above. By all means, be as liberal and expressive as you want in your interior decoration: this is your personal space. But bear in mind all the people who have to view your house from the outside, when it comes to choosing colour for the exterior. After all, you don't have to look at it most of the time! The French building colourist, Jean-Pierre Lenclos famously said: 'If you want to paint the outside of your house, get your neighbours to choose the colour'.

Below: Denys and Marjorie chose Keims silicate paint pigmented with earth colours to integrate their house with its environment.

One way of avoiding any controversy here (and indeed, it is the technique that many clever architects apply to incorporate new buildings into a community) is to use local colour. Wherever you are, the context of your house matters. Not the site itself or the location, but the context: the geology on which it sits, local flora and fauna, neighbouring buildings, communities, and so on. In fact, context is one of the issues covered by Local Agenda 21, which talks about sustainability in more than just the green sense. It also refers to the sustainability of communities.

One obvious architectural way in which a community can develop and retain a sense of identity is by using a recognizable range of building materials that are local to a place. In many parts of the country, stone walls and tiled roofs give this strong local character. In Rob Roy and Alida Saunders' case, they designed their eco-house in the style of a traditional Suffolk boarded house, ensuring that even the roof pitch was in keeping with this. Denys and Marjorie Randolph's oak-framed house also sensitively reflected local building styles by careful choice of tile, weatherboarding and render colour. Their overall design was very contemporary, yet it managed to accommodate many local vernacular elements.

Going Against the Grain

Of course, many of the buildings in the series flaunted an arrogant disregard for any kind of local traditional elements. Michael Hird and Lindsay Harwood actively fought their local council's attempts to make them use brick (a much-used material in the vicinity), choosing render instead. Sarah and Jeremy's design was deliberately avant-garde and confrontational, but in fact won the hearts of the planning authority, which thought it strikingly different and an excellent foil for the traditional housing in the adjacent conservation area. In Andrew and Deborah's case, local concerns about the future of the water tower meant that their case was going to be heard favourably by the community, even though the planning department consistently refused their applications! In any case, their design for the extension, although very modern, was hidden behind grass banks as discreetly as you can possibly imagine.

Jane Fitzsimon and Gavin Allen's build represents an interesting compromise between the freedom of contemporary architecture and the traditional vernacular values of local building styles. Their architect, David Sheppard, designed a radical structure that 'floated' inside the original chapel shell with minimal disruption. All new structural works went on in the newly dug basement while, in contrast, the exterior was sensitively restored with the correct traditional windows, pointing and paint colour. David is famous for his striking, sometimes organic designs that, at the same time, pay homage to local building materials and styles. The visual language and approach that he has developed represents the finest combination of contemporary vibrant design with respect for the vernacular. It is an exciting way forward for rural building.

Modifying Your Ideas

When it comes to adapting your design to fit in with the local vocabulary, one easy method for doing this, that you should not ignore, is the use of applied local colour in the form of paint. Although we are way behind other European countries (such as France) in this, all over Britain, village and town communities are beginning to think of their own local character in terms of a palette of paint colours that can be used to give the community a strong visual identity. Paint is a cheap and quick way of achieving this, for old buildings as well as new.

Look at houses in your area (especially old, neglected ones) to see how woodwork and walls were traditionally treated. In the past, many houses were limewashed (a porous, external coating that sparkles, unlike any modern plastic paint) and this was often coloured with locally derived powdered clay (earth pigment). Another investigative route for you to take is to see whether there are any strongly coloured clays in local streams, rivers or steep banks. Traditionally, most vernacular paints were coloured with pigments from the area, which meant that the outside appearance of buildings was used to integrate them into the landscape. At the very least, this is a useful trick for preventing a new build from shrieking out its brash presence.

Exterior Paints

If you've used render on the outside of your building, it's generally a good idea to apply limewash on top, since the slight translucency gives a wall a soft, gentle appearance as opposed to the way in which cement and plastic paints can lend a 'hard' look. On porous, lime-based renders that can 'breathe', you should only use a micro-porous coating like limewash. If you prefer to use cement-based renders and still want a more natural finish, consider white cement, to which you can add a wide range of earth colours in the cement mixer. The resulting effects can be excellent and you can even achieve a wide range of colours by experimenting with different sands, most of which are strongly pigmented with coloured clays when they are dug up!

Denys and Marjorie chose Keim's silicate paint for their render. Unlike conventional paints, this is not bound with a medium. Instead, it chemically bonds with the surface of plaster or render and dries to give a smooth finish that resembles modern coatings. Its manufacture (in Germany) is a green process; the dried coating 'breathes' like limewash and the collection is pigmented with a wide range of earth colours.

Landscaping

Having settled on your outside colour scheme, it's now time to embark on that landscaping programme that you dreamed up in the distant design days of the past. It may be that you've already made a start in a fenced-off section of the site, but much of the land around your house will still look as though a bomb has hit it. The worst of the rubble should have been removed during the build or used as hardcore as Denys and Marjorie were able to do for their terrace.

All the self-builders in the series approached the landscaping of their projects as being not only related to, but also part of, the building's design. Many of them are creating their outdoor spaces not just as external rooms, but also as gardens

and courtyards that reflect the same ethos that determines the building. So Andrew's scheme is an enclosed terrace occupying the space outside one glass wall, which is sheltered by the same earth bank as the house, and Rob and Alida's garden is laid out according to the same bio-dynamic principles as their eco-home. In this way, the Hedgehog Housing Co-op are sharing their outdoor spaces as well as their build, while Jane and Gavin have incorporated a sunken indoor 'heavenly' garden into their chapel conversion.

Denys and Marjorie's approach is as radical as anyone else's. Their 'garden' is not the landscaped acre of flower beds and lawns that we might have seen twenty years ago. Instead they are containing their formal pond and formal garden on the terrace, directly in front of the house. This structured layout is incorporated as part of the design of the building, sitting directly in front of the atrium as a 'party space' – Denys and Marjorie's own indoor/outdoor room, if you like. Beyond it lies something quite different: a vast organic meadow to be managed by Marjorie as a wild flower site (and cut by Denys), together with Denys's wildlife pond.

Achieving Harmony

Of course, your thoughts about the garden may have had to change if, like Tim Cox and Julia Brock, you have accumulated a vast mound of clay from the foundations. During the build they had not given the garden any proper consideration until they settled on reinforcing the 'house as a beach hut' idea by literally bringing the beach into the garden in the form of tons of pebbles, shells and

decking to echo the tide breaks down below. The couple have turfed over their 'neolithic tumulus' of clay and now plan to plant dozens of native species trees on the site to ensure that the house will eventually blend into its surroundings. It is total serendipity, but now that the garden is laid out, their undulating tumulus appropriately resembles the shape of sand dunes.

Top, middle and above: Denys and Marjorie's wild flower meadow will take time to mature, although they know there are many species present. Denys's pond needs some work before it finally takes shape.

Below: Decoration doesn't have to be confined to the inside. The 'beach hut' theme extends to the exterior at Newhaven.

Of course trees will eventually hide any building and help to render it anonymous and acceptable in any community, but many architects consider them to be only a 'get-out' clause, a way of covering up mistakes. As Roderick James is fond of quoting: 'A doctor can bury his mistakes, an architect can merely plant vines'. At its best, planting will harmonize with a building, not envelop it. Think of Jane and Gavin's new orchards below their chapel or, again, Denys and Marjorie's meadow. This kind of sensitivity to the garden in relation to the house, in relation to the environment and in relation to the surrounding landscape, illustrates an important change. It shows that garden and landscape design in Britain is undergoing a renaissance, being driven not by the whims of designers but by the excitement of new homeowners and their philosophies. It also goes to show that when anyone embarks on building a dream house, what then follows is a radical approach to the garden as well.

Decorating

And so, finally, some words about turning your interior spaces into rooms in which you can live. This is where you can put into practice all the ideas that you've been saving up to achieve a mood and style that you've always dreamed of. It's these touches that will imprint your personality on your home and make it yours, and not the architect's or builder's.

Don't rush to get things done. It takes time to get used to a new home as you fumble for the light switch and try to open unfamiliar doors in the wrong way. We always underestimate the myriad tiny ways in which we have instinctively learnt all the little details of how our home works, and so it's not surprising that it takes

several months before you can feel entirely at ease in a new place. It's important that details, such as door catches and switches, work not only for the house but also for you. In these tiny elements the true ergonomics of a building are tested and this example represents one of the major contributions that an architect, when involved from the start of the project, can make to your daily life.

Bright Ideas

A very important aspect of the design to be considered is lighting. Many of the self-builders in the series began, as they should, by thinking about lighting at the design stage of the project – by talking to their architect about it and planning the wiring layouts from the outset (see Chapter 3, Design for Living, pages 54–71). It's as well to be as flexible as possible in your planning and to allow for pendant fittings, wall lights and hidden lighting, as well as 5-amp socket circuits to take table lamps

that can be switched on from a normal wall-mounted switch. Dimmers on every circuit are essential and low-voltage lighting should be used with discrimination (it works particularly well in kitchens and bathrooms).

Above: Details like these in Denys and Marjorie's home make all the difference to the finished look.

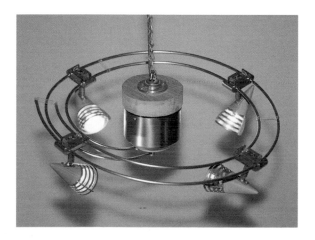

Think about using lighting to uplight ceilings and to wash the walls to provide gentle, ambient light that will make the rooms seem larger and more relaxing. Position wall lights sufficiently high so that if you install uplighters, they don't shine in your eyes. As a general principle, glare is the most uncomfortable element in poor lighting, so

Left: There's a great variety of lighting available which can create different effects depending on the room's use and position. This unusual light fitting hangs above Denys and Marjorie's bed.

avoid it at all costs by hiding bulbs, directing light, using opaque shades on worklamps and fitting large, diffusing shades over naked bulbs. Consider too, the need to light your garden and building exterior, and the possibility of using energy-saving fixtures here (and elsewhere). They do not need to be solely fluorescent forms of lighting. You can light areas outside using metal halide (white), mercury (pale blue) or high-pressure sodium (pink) lighting, rather as they do in public areas.

Colour

If you don't have strong ideas about colour schemes, then consider studying how colour works a little more. Books on colour psychology offer fascinating insights into how we perceive and respond to colour. Red, for example, raises blood pressure and the production of adrenalin, making it an ideal shade for a room in which you socialize, such as the dining room. By contrast, it would be disastrous in a bedroom, where light blue (for calmness) or green (for balance) would certainly work better.

Whatever your plans, it is never a bad idea to paint the whole house out in white or off-white, to live in it for a while and then to start planning. After all, you are not an interior designer with a deadline to meet and it is likely that your mind has been less than focused on the interior decoration during the previous months. Very

few of us are endowed with a strong spatial sense that allows us to imagine a space in detail, so it is important not to be too rigid when thinking ahead as to how the project will look when it is finished. It is better to wait for inspiration to build up slowly in your mind once you have moved in.

Examples of Colour Schemes

Many self-builders have very clear views right from the beginning as to how their space will look when it is completed. Jane and Gavin always intended to use rich earth colours – terracottas and ochres – between the chapel's timber beams, and as the build progressed and they could see the internal structures developing, they were both able to plan the colour scheme in more detail. Sarah and Jeremy (and Michael and Lindsey) envisaged clean, white interiors accented with bright colours on one or two walls. This aesthetic is a popular one at the moment; it incorporates colour in a safe, contained way while retaining a pared-back overall look.

More adventurous altogether were Rob and Alida. Alida devised an overall scheme of warm tones with certain areas allocated to much stronger hues. Whether this scheme works is not simply a question of judgement, it is also a matter of personal taste. If you are happy with a scheme, if it has been executed with skill and entered into with gusto, then you have every right to proclaim it a success, regardless of what anyone else thinks of it. Although exterior paint schemes are open to the criticism of the entire world, your interior decoration is, by contrast, a very personal affair.

Overall Design

How you cover the walls will largely dictate the feel of a room. Since your home has just been built, any plastered walls need to be left to dry out thoroughly before any wallpapering can take place and this means months, not days. Fortunately, a ready alternative to this is paint. The right type – distemper, limewash, casein paint, silicate paint or

Below: Tim and Julia's children love bold colours.

even the cheapest trade emulsion (which is surprisingly porous) – will allow walls to breathe and dry out, transpiring moisture through the coating layer. Paint is also a relatively quick form of decoration: it is the simplest way of introducing colour, and it is also cheap and easily changed.

The use of paint, wallcoverings, flooring, furniture and soft furnishings all have a powerful impact on the general design of your interiors, especially when those interiors present themselves as an empty shell or blank canvas. Tim and Julia's house, although of timber construction, was made from pre-fab panels that were clad both internally and externally. The result inside gave plaster-finished walls and ceilings that betrayed no idea of how the building had been constructed, giving the couple total freedom to create any interior design they wanted.

Complementary Schemes

However, there are many building types and construction methods that dictate an aesthetic, inside as much as out. Denys and Marjorie's oak barn has, arguably, a

Above: In this Carpenter Oak interior the beautiful, natural tones of the wood set the colour scheme for the whole room.

bigger design impact on the interior than the exterior; all the beams are visible and are left, in the time-honoured manner, in the raw. This means that any decorative scheme must not only complement the huge quantity of pale-coloured oak that is visible, it must also stand up to the chunky style of the wood. The Walter Segal houses, built by the Hedgehog Housing Co-op, also imposed their own look on the interiors. These wooden-built structures are made mainly of pine, which is present indoors in the form of beams and posts. Because it is not intrinsically as beautiful a wood as oak, there is an argument for treating it with stain and colour. This is something that we tried to do in the series in an effort to move Segal interiors away from the rather fossilized 1970s look that they have always had in the past.

Contemporary materials also make themselves felt indoors. The huge glass walls of Andrew and Deborah's house imposed their own kind of transparent aesthetic on the interiors, allowing light and the outside world to flood indoors. This same principle applied to Michael and Lindsay's home, which was built from huge glass sheets, and also to Sarah and Jeremy's build in Islington. Indeed, their interior design ideas seem to be based on principles of transparency as the exterior where some walls are glass and much of the building is made of straw that is kept visible by a great wall of polycarbonate sheeting.

In Conclusion

If there is one fear to allay, one general point to make about the decoration, design and even the 'completion' of your home, it is that no house is ever truly finished.

Below: The attractive beams used in the construction of Denys and Marjorie's house have a strong impact on the interior of their home and in some places have made it difficult to know how best to position their collection of paintings.

We are conditioned – by magazines, by advertising and by television – to think of homes as being perfect places that are constantly in a state of being primped and tidied in readiness for the photographer's arrival. It is a sad reflection of our values that the goal for many amateur decorators is to have their home featured in some monthly magazine. In truth, homes are not really like that at all. They are often untidy, relaxed and flexible places, sometimes with a room or two whose function is fuzzy, or in transition. And that is how they should be: homes, not room

sets. The best houses are those with fuzziness (or flexibility, to put it another way) built in, that allows for the building's changing uses over the years. As children grow up, as we become old and as customs change, we will inevitably want to use a building in different ways.

The problem of changing use (and frustration with how traditional houses are laid out) has led many people to the idea of self-building a house to suit the way in which we live nowadays. This book has followed a number of inspired individuals who have done just that. By reading about real cases and about real people who have put themselves on the line to achieve what only a small number of people in this country have done, you may feel encouraged to join them. Whatever your circumstances, if you are prepared to devote yourself and your time tirelessly to such a project, then building your own dream home is something that really is within your grasp. Good luck!

Above: Marjorie Randolph's plant containers, still waiting to be moved to their new home.

Checklists

CHAPTER 1: FINDING A SITE

Where to Look

- Estate agents
- Local and national newspapers
- Self-build magazines
- Plot-finding agencies
- Adverts in local press
- Adverts in local builders' merchants
- Local farmers, architects, surveyors, solicitors
- Local amenities companies or the Church
- Ordnance Survey map
- Kit-home companies
- Local planning office
- 'For Sale' signs
- Use your own imagination
- Properties up for conversion

What to Watch Out For

- Sloping ground
- Trees
- Ground conditions
- Access to mains services
- Access to land/visibility splays
- Ransom strips
- Covenants
- Easements
- Public footpaths
- Boundaries
- Planning permission

How to Buy

- Exchange and completion of contracts through solicitor
- Take an option
- Auctions – go to a few of these first, but don't get auction fever. Stick to your price limit
- By tender

CHAPTER 2: DO YOU NEED AN ARCHITECT?

How to Find One

- Through television or magazines
- In the family
- Personal recommendation
- Through the package company
- RIBA client advisory service
- Association of Self-build Architects
- *Yellow Pages*

Finding Out More About Them

- Registration with ARB
- Study their previous work
- Talk to recent clients
- Compatibility
- Ask about their fees

The Role of the Client

- Discuss your needs and requirements in detail
- Provide sketches
- Keep a scrapbook
- Be clear about your budget

What a Good Architect Will Do

- Initial drawings and models
- Submission of detailed drawings for planning permission and building regulations
- Prepare specifications for tender
- Assist in cutting back to meet the budget
- Recommend relevant specialists

- Manage the project
- Issue certificates when payment is due to contractors
- Understand space and how it is used
- Communicate to you how the building will look, and take you through the whole planning and building process

CHAPTER 3: DESIGN FOR LIVING

Acknowledge your Lifestyle

- Open-plan or traditional?
- Are you tidy or not?
- Choose your rooms/areas and how they relate to one another
- Television, lighting and electrical sockets
- Allow for future development
- Space for personal belongings

Consider your site

- Views and direction
- Impact on the local environment
- Sensitivity to existing building if converting
- Outside buildings
- Landscaping

CHAPTER 4: MATERIAL FACTS

What to Consider

- The design of your home
- How you plan to use it
- How eco-friendly you want to be
- Where it is located
- Local planners may have particular requirements if you are in a conservation area
- Make sure window frames, doors and roof complement body of your home

- Get samples of all material to make sure they work well together

Building With Brick

- Stock bricks – made from good quality clay and have a good finish
- Common bricks – made to less high standards and used where they can't be seen
- Breeze blocks/lightweight 'blown cement' blocks – generally used where not seen
- Sand-faced flettons – common brick with special facing on one side, giving the look without the expense
- Bricks give sense of solidity and permanence
- Different combinations of brick and tile can transform the exterior of a building

Building With Timber Frames

- Speed – timber-panelled kit homes can be fabricated off-site and erected in a matter of days
- Usually involves fewer people on site
- Can avoid brickwork if the outer wall is timber too
- Avoids use of wet trades
- Wide choice of timber-panelled kit homes available
- Cheap
- Pleasant to handle
- No need for expensive machinery and the skills that go with it
- Aesthetically pleasing to the eye and can be combined with more modern materials for effect
- Can be grown sustainably
- Has low embodied energy
- Extremely energy efficient

- Excellent insulation
- Durable
- Requires low level of maintenance

Building Underground

- Low visual impact
- Low maintenance costs
- Stability in temperature levels
- Protection from extreme weather conditions
- Insulating properties of turf roofs

Building With Straw Bales

- Originated as building material in 1840s Nebraska, USA
- Concerns of fire risks and pests have been proven unfounded
- Need to take care to prevent damp and mould
- Sustainable
- Low embodied energy
- Cheap

Building With Cob

- Mud and straw
- Similar advantages to straw

Building with Glass

- Beginning to find a foothold in domestic architecture
- Manufacture in increased spans means it can work as a structural element and work as a wall
- Double- or triple- glazing can ensure efficient insulation
- Opens the home to the outside world
- Can be effectively combined with more traditional materials for superb effects
- Privacy might be a problem!

CHAPTER 5: GET PLANNING

Planning Officers' Concerns

- How the building fits into its environment
- Siting of the building
- Compatibility with neighbouring buildings
- Proposed materials
- Access
- Whether it's in a conservation area
- Whether there is a change of use involved
- How will it affect the density of population

Three Kinds of Planning Permission

- Outline – land is approved for development – lasts three years
- Approval of reserved matters – follows submission of detailed plans
- Detailed or full permission i.e. combination of above lasts five years

What the Planners Must See

- A location plan (from Ordnance Survey 1:1250 or 1:2500)
- An existing site plan, showing any existing buildings, trees, telegraph poles etc.

What the Planners Also Want to See For Reserved Matters or Detailed Permission

- A proposed site plan with the footprint of your building clearly marked showing access route and any trees that may need to be felled (1:500 or 1:200)
- Detailed floorplans (1:100 or 1:50)
- Elevations of the front, back and sides of the house (1:100 or 1:50)
- Details of the materials you propose to use for your build

What To Do If You Don't Receive a Reply

- Contact the planning officer and discuss your plans, though he is not obliged to do this
- Employ a planning consultant who knows their way through the labyrinth of planning rules and regulations
- Prepare a scaled-down model of the proposed building
- Prepare a written justification of what you propose
- Canvas for local support
- Be co-operative in answering inquiries from neighbours, however hostile

What To Do If Permission is Refused

- Reapply with compromise solutions
- Appeal to the Secretary of State in writing

But BEWARE, this can be costly, time-consuming and disheartening

Building Regulations

After your application to the council, the building inspector will pay a number of visits to your site at key stages to ensure that the building is structurally sound.

CHAPTER 6: MONEY MATTERS

How Much Money Will You Need?

- Cost of the land
- Outside costs – solicitor, architect, planning consultant, quantity surveyor, structural engineer, soil engineer, site manager
- Any other professional fees, including labour costs (if you are managing the project yourself)
- Planning permission
- Building regulations and inspections
- Cost of building society loan

- Valuation fees
- Warranties
- Mains connection fees (gas, water, electricity, phone)
- Septic tank, mini-treatment centre, cesspit, composting toilet, reed beds
- Driveway/access to site
- Insurances
- Accommodation
- Landscaping
- Garage/tool shed
- Phone/fax/travel
- At least ten per cent contingency

Building Costs

- Using detailed plans and written specifications, approach builders' merchants, quantity surveyor or separate sub-contractors for estimates on materials
- Labour

How to Get Your Estimates Down

- Omit certain features
- Do some of the work yourself
- Live on the site
- Scale down the size

Sources of Money

- Private funds
- Bank
- Building society
- Building co-operative

CHAPTER 7: MAKING IT HAPPEN

Who Can Manage the Project

- Your architect

- A main contractor
- A project manager
- You

How to Choose and Use a Main Contractor

- Go by personal recommendation if you can
- Interview three or four potential builders and ask for quotes on the job after you've supplied them with detailed drawings and a written specification
- Look at some of their latest work
- Talk to recent clients
- Don't agree to anything that you don't fully understand
- Use a contract

What the builder's contract should include

- Start and finish dates
- Provisos in case you change your mind
- All extra costs should be agreed in writing
- Payment schedule
- Retention sum
- What happens if the builder dies or disappears
- Detailed plans and specifications (attached)

What To Do If You Are The Project Manager

- Make sure that you are as thoroughly versed in the process as possible, by reading and talking to those who know
- Target key stages of the build
- Work out systems for security, safety, paying the workers, insurance, filing, VAT, ordering materials, scheduling deliveries and book keeping

Pitfalls

- Non-delivery of materials

- Disappearance of sub-contractors to another job
- Not checking the work thoroughly
- Disorganization

CHAPTER 8: HOW GREEN CAN YOU GO?

- Find materials with low-embodied energy that are manufactured using low-polluting, low-cost methods. Good examples include softwoods and hardwoods from managed sources, straw bale, cob, lime mortar, distemper and organic paints. Concrete has surprisingly low-embodied energy relative to the poor scorers – brick, tile, glass and steel.
- Part of a material's embodied energy is measured by how far it has to travel to arrive on site. The further it is, the greater the embodied energy. Liquids are particularly costly to transport, so consider mixing all your wet stuff on site – concrete, plasters and even paints. Many green paint suppliers deliver water-based paints in powder form.
- Structural materials with high thermal mass can be used to minimize heat loss in a house: internal stone and brick walls, painted in dark colours near a window, will absorb infra-red and act as giant radiators at night. Additionally materials such as straw bales, that have high insulative values, will keep the heat in.
- There is often a compromise to be brokered between traditional methods and materials and modern technology which carries with it the associated high capital costs of many modern materials, both financially and in terms of the manufacturing processes' pollution and embodied energy. Solvent-free acrylic paints

may be user-friendly but they are still petroleum products which pollute in the factory and which are wastefully shipped across the country in liquid form. Pilkington K glass is also expensive and energy-heavy to produce, but it has excellent properties for retaining and trapping solar infra-red energy in a building. To achieve practicable greenness sometimes means using products such as these.

- Recycling applies to capital materials as well as consumables. There is a ready market in second-hand building materials and gash timber (builders' seconds). In addition, recycling can be built into the house – heat exchangers, secondary heat coils in boiler flues, composting toilets, reed-beds for grey water effluent, catchment of rainwater from roofs, etc.

- To conserve as much of the existing environment as possible, it helps to build houses with 'light footprints' that consume the minimum of natural materials in their construction and which cover the smallest surface area on the plot. This is achievable by burying homes, giving them turf roofs and constructing them on concrete piles, rather than floated concrete bases and foundations.

- Building an eco-friendly house does not require a change of lifestyle or imply that you've dropped out. Green details can be easily and pragmatically incorporated into any building and will usually result in your saving money. Remember that working to conserve the environment is no longer a fad or the role of the eco-warrior. It now forms a core part of the planning policy of any local authority through Local Agenda 21.

CHAPTER 9: FINISHING TOUCHES

Consider the Environment

- The interior of our home – it's essential to provide a pleasing surrounding in which we can flourish
- The built environment – how does your building fit in to its surroundings?
- The natural environment – make environmentally friendly choices which may reflect the area in which you're building, particularly with regard to the local architectural vernacular or colour palette

Interior decorating

- Take your time before making radical decisions
- Lighting
- Colour – choose carefully
- Let the house dictate the aesthetic
- Let the living spaces reflect your lifestyle however relaxed, flexible or untidy you may be

Appendix

Architects

Architect – Suffolk
Neil Winder
Star Yard
Millway Lane
Palgrave
Norfolk IP22 1AD
01379 641592

Architect – Newhaven
Hardy Associates
38 Queen Square
Bristol BS1 4QS
0500 070554

Architect – Cornwall
David Sheppard
49 Fore Street
Plympton
St Maurice
Plymouth PL7 3RZ
01752 336333

Architect - Brighton
Bob Hayes
Robin Hillier (Project Architect)
Architype
The Morocco Store
1 Leathermarket Street
London SE1 3HN
0171 403 2889
Fax 0171 407 5283
Website www.architype.co.uk

Architects - Islington
Sarah Wigglesworth and Jeremy Till
9 Stock Orchard Street
London N7 9RW
0171 607 9200
01302 721071

Architect – Oxfordshire
Roderick James
Laurence Burrell (Project Architect)
Carpenter Oak & Woodland Co. Ltd
The Framing Yard
East Cornworthy
Totnes
Devon TQ9 7HF
01803 732900
Fax 01803 732901

Architectural designer – Doncaster
Colin Harwood
111 Bennetthorpe Road
Doncaster DN2 6AD
0797 985 0545
E-mail colinharwood@hotmail.com

Architect – Amersham
Andrew Tate
Tate & Hindle Design Ltd
Ramillies Building
215 Oxford Street
London W1R 1AG
0171 287 2412

Engineers and Consultants

Structural Engineer – Doncaster
Blackwood Structural Design
14 Kennedy Street
Manchester M2 4BY
0161 228 2610

Structural Engineer – Doncaster
Graham Fletcher & Associates
Enniskerry House
Glen Road
Doncaster DN3 3NN
01302 536577

Planning consultant – Doncaster
John Hunt
Hall Cottage
Old Skellow
Doncaster DN6 8JR

Quantity surveyor – Coleshill
Gardiner &Theobald
32 Bedford Square
London WC1B 3EG
0171 209 3000

Structural engineer – Coleshill

WSP
Vantage House
1 Weir Road
Wimbledon SW19 8UX
0181 266 3000

Structural Engineers – Islington
Nick Hanika, Andy Heyne and Richard Seville
Price & Myers
33–34 Alfred Place
London WC1E 7DP
0171 631 5128
Fax 0171 436 4905
Employed to solve the problem of the adjacent railway line using giant springs to soak up vibration and reduce noise.

Accoustic consultant – Islington
Paul Gillieron Accoustics
130a Brixton Hill
London SW2 1AH
0181 671 2223
Fax 0181 671 2402

Contract management – Islington
Martin Hughes
Koya Construction Ltd
84 Furley Rd
London SE15 1UG
0171 639 6255
Fax 0171 277 7918

Additional framework design – Suffolk
Sidney Palmer
Hillhouse
Minto
Hawick
Borders TD9 8SB
01450 870466

Engineer – Suffolk
John Allen Associates
1 The Link
New Ash Green
Kent DA3 8HG
01474 872274

Building Suppliers And Materials

Maritex fabric cladding – Islington
Alpha
Sherborne
Dorset DT9 3RB
01935 813722
Fax 01935 811800

Concrete blocks/thermal consultants – Doncaster
Durox Building Products Ltd
Linford Plant
Stanford-Le-Hope
Essex SS17 0PY
01375 656241

External chimney – Doncaster
Selkirk Ltd
Pottington Industrial Estate
Barnstaple
Devon EX31 1LZ
01271 326633
Website www.selkirk.co.uk

Internal chimney – Doncaster
Isokern UK
14 Haviland Road
Ferndown Industrial Estate
Wimborne
Dorset BH21 7FR
01202 861650
E-mail info@isokern.co.uk
Website www.isokern.co.uk

External ramps – Doncaster
Eurogrid
British Industrial Engineering (Staffs) Ltd
Halesfield 19
Telford
Shropshire TF7 4QT
01952 581988
E-mail sales@eurogrid.co.uk

Expamet – Doncaster
Expamet Building Products
PO Box 52

Longhill Industrial Estate
Hartlepool TS25 1PR
01429 866611

Basement waterproofing – Doncaster

Ruberoid Building Products Ltd
14 Tewin Road
Welwyn Garden City
Hertfordshire AL7 1BP
01707 822222

Kal-Zip aluminum roof – Doncaster

Hoogovens Aluminium Building
  Systems
Haydock Lane
Haydock
Merseyside WA11 9TY
01942 295500
Website www.hoogovens.co.uk

Roofing fitters – Doncaster

Bennett & Cunningham
Beaufort Street
St Helens
Merseyside WA9 3BJ
01744 451081

Anti-vibration springs – Islington

Gerb
Sylviastrasse 21
45131 Essen
Germany
Fax: 00 49 201 2660 450
Steel springs used to solve the
problem of extreme vibration caused
by the adjacent railway tracks.

Straw bales – Islington

Abbott & Co.
Abbersley House
Park Street
Cirencester
Gloucestershire GL17 2BX
01285 653738
Fax 01285 885134

Masonite framework – Suffolk

distributed by:
Fillcrete Ltd
Grindell Street
Hull HU9 1RT
01482 223405

represented by:
Panel Agency Ltd
Maple House
5 Over Minnis
New Ash Green
Longfield
Kent DA3 8JA
01474 872578
Swedish eco-friendly wood-frames
material.

Panalvent/Masonite/ Warmcel – Brighton

Fillcrete Ltd
Grindell Street
Hull HU9 1RT
01482 223405
Fax 01482 327957

Gabions – Islington

Maccaferri
Leyden Road
Stevenage
Hertfordshire SG1 2BP
01438 315504
Fax 01438 740335
Wire cages filled with recycled
stones, as used on motorways.

Timber trusses – Islington

Cox Long Ltd
Airfield Industrial Estate
Hixon
Staffordshire ST18 0PA
01889 270166
Fax 01889 271041
Used for straw-bale wall.

Scaffolding – Newhaven

Safeguard Scaffolds
8a Shaftsbury Place
Brighton
East Sussex BN1 4QS
01273 674336

Sockets – Doncaster

Caradon MK Electric Ltd
The Arnold Centre
Paycocke Road
Basildon
Essex SS14 3EA
01268 563000

Reclaimed railway sleepers – Newhaven

Romsey Reclamation

Station Approach
Romsey
Hampshire SO51 8DU
01794 524174

Flooring – Doncaster

Richard Lees Ltd
Weston Underwood
Ashbourne
Derbyshire DE6 4PH
01335 360601
Fax 01335 360014

Exterior paint – Oxfordshire

Keim Mineral Paints Ltd
Muckley Cross
Morville
Shropshire WV16 4RR
01746 714543
Fax 01746 714526

Precast concrete slabs – Coleshill

Bison Concrete Products Ltd
Amington House
Silica Road
Tamworth
Staffordshire B77 4DT
01827 641641

Fillmaster – Coleshill

Vencel Resil Ltd
Arndale House
18–20 Spital Street
Dartford
Kent DA1 2HT
01322 626600
Bulky polystyrene product used for
landscaping.

Timber floor – Coleshill

Junckers Ltd
Wheaton Cork Commercial Centre
Whitham
Essex CM83 EUJ
01376 517512

Cement – Suffolk

Lafarge Redland Aggregates Ltd
Wallace House
4 Falcon Way
Shire Park
Welwyn Garden City
Hertfordshire AL7 1TW
01707 356024

Damp-proofing material – Suffolk

Zedcore Ltd
Zedcore Business Park
Bridge Street
Witney
Oxfordshire OX8 6LJ
01993 776346

Cedar roof shingles – Suffolk

John Brash Timber
The Old Ship Yard
Gainsborough
Lincolnshire DN21 1NG
01427 613858

Wallform – Coleshill

Beco Products Ltd
Beco House
Wrawby Road
Brigg
Lincolnshire DN20 8DT
01652 651641

Green roof system– Coleshill

Euroroof
White House Works
Bold Road
Sutton
St Helens
Merseyside WA9 4JG
01744 820103

Concrete reinforcements and formers – Suffolk

Prepour Services
Unit 6
Lion Barn Industrial Estate
Needham Market
Suffolk IP6 8NZ
01449 722181

Recycled hardwood ring beams – Suffolk

Ashwell Recycling
Unit G
Criton Industrial Estate
Stanford Road
Orsett
Essex RM16 3BH
01375 892576

Gilding – Newhaven

Guilders Warehouse
Unit 5
Woodside Commercial Estate
Thornwood
Epping
Essex CM16 6LJ
01992 570453
Brass transfer metal, a cheap
substitute for gold leaf.

Flooring – Newhaven

Granite, Marble & Stone
Unit 7
Crown Yard
Bedgebury Road
Goudhurst
Kent TN17 2QZ
01580 212222

Expamet – Doncaster

Expamet Building Products
PO Box 52
Longhill Industrial Estate
Hartlepool TS25 1PR
01429 866611

Carlite browning/external render – Doncaster

British Gypsum
Head Office
East Leake
Loughborough
Leicestershire LE12 6HX
0990 456 1230

Rubberfuse roof covering – Islington

Integrated Polymer Systems
Thornton Rust Hall
Thornton Rust
Leyburn
North Yorkshire BL8 3AW
01709 581000
Fax 01969 663000

Water Garden Services – Brighton

Inetrpret Ltd
Vincent lane
Dorking
Surrey RH4 3YX
01306 885009

Builders And Craftsmen

Eco-builders' merchants – Suffolk

Joe Hilton
Eco Merchant Ltd
The Old Filling Station
Head Hill Road
Goodnestone
Kent ME13 9BY
01795 530130

Kit-house project management – Newhaven

Unique Homes
38 Queen Square
Bristol BS1 4QS
Website www.uniquehomes.co.uk

Pilebreaker – Cornwall

Pilebreaker Ltd
Sunstone House
School Lane
Plympton-St-Maurice
Devon PL7 1NQ
01752 336407

Carpenter – Newhaven

Malcolm Streeter
11 Wellesley Close
Cooden
Bexhill-On-Sea
East Sussex TN39 3PX
01424 845360

Windows – Newhaven

Atlas Building & Maintenance
Whitehouse Farm
30 Pembury Grove
Bexhill-On-Sea
East Sussex TN39 4BT
01424 211951

Kit-house construction – Newhaven

Hurst Carpentry Ltd
Old Court Cottage
Staunton-on-Arrow
Herefordshire HR6 9HR
01544 388941

Plumber/underfloor heating – Newhaven

Option Heating

8 Arun Road
Bognor Regis
West Sussex PO21 5PD
01243 860487

Electrician – Newhaven

Amber Services
Steve Heselden
104 Whitley Road
Eastbourne BN22 8ND
01323 638610

Building contractor – Amersham

Jesse Mead Ltd
176 Berkhampstead Road
Chesham HP5 3EU
01494 784611

Equipment

Bomag 80 roller – Newhaven

Cox Hire Centres
Marchants Way
Sheddingdean Industrial Estate
Burgess Hill
West Sussex RH15 8QY
01444 247878
Rollers to flatten uneven surfaces like
driveways, and other building
materials for hire.

Electronic roller shutters – Doncaster

Industrial Doors
Unit 8
11 Victoria Road
Doncaster DN6 7AZ
01302 337547

Nail guns – Brighton

ITW Passlode
Queensway
Ffortfach
Swansea SA5 4ED

Drills – Brighton

De Walt Uk
210 Bath Road
Slough
Berkshire SL1 3YD
01753 567055
Fax 01753 572112

Landscaping and Garden Equipment

Landscape architect – all builds

Johnny Rath
Oast House
Isnage Farm
Bentley
Surrey GU10 5LX
01420 23728

Beach pebbles and sub-base - Newhaven

Hall Aggregates (South Coast)
North Quay Road
Newhaven
East Sussex BN9 0AB
01273 514917
Removing shingle from beaches is
illegal, but substitutes are available.

Turf – Newhaven

Rolawn (Turf-Growers) Ltd
Elvington
York YO41 4XR
01904 608661

Earthworks equipment – Newhaven

Karren Plant Hire
11 Solway Avenue
Patcham
Brighton BN1 8UJ
01273 883699

Earthworks equipment – Brighton

Harman Plant Hire Ltd.
The Hyde
Bevendean Industrial Estate
Brighton BN2 4JE
01273 603021

Top-soil – Newhaven

F. L. Gamble & Son
Meadow Road Industrial Estate
Worthing
West Sussex BN11 2RY
01273 612366

Plants – Newhaven

Architectural Plants
Cooks Farm
Nuthurst

Horsham
West Sussex RH13 6LH
01403 891772

Perryhill Nurseries
Hartfield
East Sussex TN7 4JP
01892 770377

Plumbing and Drainage

Condensing boiler – Newhaven and Amersham
Eco Hometec (UK) Ltd
22–24 Scot Lane
Doncaster DN1 1ES
01302 769769

Civic drain – Doncaster
Aco Drain
Hitchin Road
Shefford
Bedfordshire SG17 6TE
01462 816666
E-mail drainsales@aco.co.uk
Website www.aco.co.uk/drain

Septic tank – Cornwall
Klargester
Enviromental Engineering Ltd
College Road
Aston Clinton
Buckinghamshire HP22 5EW
01296 633000
Fax 01296 633001
Website www.klargester.co.uk
E-mail uksales@klargester.co.uk
Send SAE for *The Off-mains (Drainage) Guide Site Assessment And System Selection*

Plumbing – Cornwall
John Bull
Hepworth Flexible Plumbing
Hazelhead
Crow Edge
Sheffield S36 4HG
01226 763561
Fax 01226 765110

Ifo low-flush toilets – Islington
Elemental Solutions
01981 540 728
Fax 01981 541044

Oasis rainwater harvesting tanks – Islington
Albion Concrete
Pipehouse Wharf
Morfa Road
Swansea SA1 1TD
01792 655968
Fax 01792 644461

Rainwater pumps – Islington
The Green Shop
Bisley
Gloucestershire GL6 7BX
01452 770629
Fax 01452 770629

Composting toilet – Islington
Kingsley Clivius
5–7 Woodside Rd.
Eastley
Hampshire SO50 4ET
01703 615680
Fax 01703 642613

Zen solar collector for hot water – Islington
Construction Resources
16 Great Guildford Street
London SE1 0HS
0171 450 2211
Fax 0171 450 2212

Heating boiler (condenser) – Cornwall
Yorkpark Ltd.
16 St George's Industrial Estate
White Lion Road
Amersham
Buckinghamshire HP7 9JQ
01494 764031
Fax 01494 765754
E-mail sales@yorkpark.u-net.com

HDPE pipework – Suffolk
Geberit UK
Metcalfe House
25 Kirkgate
Ripon
North Yorkshire HG4 1PB
01765 602082

Downrunners – Suffolk
Dales Fabrications
Crompton Road Industrial Estate
Ilkeston
Derbyshire DE7 4BG

0115 930 1521
Nordal aluminium rainwater goods.

Biotec sewage system – Newhaven
Entec Pollution Control Ltd
West Portway
Andover SP10 3LF
01264 357666

Rainwater pump – Newhaven
Allerton
Woodbridge Road
Sleaford
Lincolnshire NG34 7EW
01529 305757

Rainwater recycling unit – Suffolk
Eco-Vat
Unit 8
Enterprise Way
Whitby Business Park
Whitby
North Yorkshire YO22 4NH
01947 600033
E-mail ecovat@aol.com

Drainage – Suffolk
Naylor Clayware
Clough Green
Cawthorne
Barnsley S75 4AD
01226 790591

Wellbutt grey water recycling system – Suffolk
Water Dynamics Ltd
Unit 32
Branbridges Industrial Estate
East Peckham
Tonbridge
Kent TN12 5HF
01622 873322

Dual-flush toilets – Suffolk
Villeroy & Boch
267 Merton Road
London SW18 5JS
0181 871 4028

Glazing

Designer – Doncaster
Roland Leopoldseder
Zeichenburo-Leopoldseder Roland
A-4300 St Valentin
Rubingerstrasse 14
Austria
00 43 7435 570 4819
zbl@magnet.at

Glass fitters/glass blocks
Roger Wilde
Chareau House
1 Miles Street
Oldham OL1 3NY
0161 624 6824

Double-glazed windows – Brighton
The Velux Company Ltd
The Barn
Cow Lane
Bushey
Hertfordshire WD2 3EL
0181 950 9922
Fax 0181 950 3707

Glazed bricks – Doncaster
Ibstock Bricks
Roughdales Ltd
Chester Lane
St Helens
Merseyside WA9 4EN
0870 903 4014

Windows and doors – Islington
Environmental Construction
  Products
26 Millmoor Road
Meltham
Huddersfield HD7 3JY
01484 854898
Fax 01484 834899
Ecoplus and natural wood stains.

Glass – Doncaster
Eckelt
18 Ristostrasse
A4400 Steyr
Austria
00 43 7252 8940

**Windows and doors –
Suffolk**
Swedish Window Company Ltd
The Airfield
Earls Colne Industrial Park
Colchester CO6 2NS
01787 223931

**Glass curtain walling –
Coleshill**
Velfac Ltd
Merlin Place
Milton Road
Cambridge CB4 0DP
01223 426606

Glazing – Brighton
Solaglass
Hartcliffe Way
Bristol BS3 5SB
0117 902 1000
Fax 0117 902 6260

Heating

**Warmcel Insulation –
Suffolk and Islington**
Excel Industries
Unit 13
Rassau Industrial Estate
Ebbw Vale
Gwent NP3 5SD
01495 350655
Fax 01495 350146

Bitvent insulation – Suffolk
Hunton Fiber (UK) Ltd
22a High Street
Irthlingborough
Northamptonshire NN9 5TN
01933 651811

**Passivent ventilation –
Suffolk**
Willan Building Services
2 Brooklands Road
Sale
Cheshire M33 3SS
0161 962 7113

Loft insulation – Newhaven
Progressive Products Ltd
Industrial Estate
Presteigne
Powys LD8 2UF
01544 260500

**Jablite polystyrene
insulation – Amersham**
Vencel Resil Ltd
Arndale House
18–20 Spital Street
Dartford
Kent DA1 2HT
01322 626600

**Claycork roof insulation -
Islington**
E. J. Clay
Clay Group House
Albert Street
Lockwood
Huddersfield HD1 3PT
01484 536531
Fax 01484 518083

**Warm water underfloor
heating – Cornwall**
Nu Heat
Unit 5
Lakes Court
Old Fore Street
Sidmouth
Devon EX10 8LP
01395 578482
Fax 01395 515502

**Heat recovery ventilation –
Islington**
Baxi Clean Air
Unit 20
Roman Way
Ribbleton Way
Preston PR2 5BB
01772 693700
Fax 01772 693701

**Underfloor heating –
Amersham**
Thermoboard
Unit 4
Fair Oak Close
Exeter Airport Business Park
Exeter
Devon EX5 2UL
01392 444122

Kitchens and Bathrooms

Kitchen – Newhaven
Winning Designs – Southern Office

'Razaal'
Stream Lane
Nutbourne
Pulborough
West Sussex RH20 2HG
07000 094664
Website www.winning-designs uk.com

Taps – Amersham
Vola UK Ltd
Unit 12
Ampthill Business Park
Station Road
Ampthill
Bedfordshire NK45 2QW
01525 841155

Villager stove – Newhaven
Lyme Regis Engineering Co. Ltd
Millwey Industrial Estate
Axminster
Devon EX13 5HU
01297 35596

**Furniture and kitchen –
Amersham**
Barn 6
Tallents Farm
Kimpton Bottom
Kimpton
Hertfordshire SG4 8EU
01438 833703

Bathroom – Cornwall
C. P. Hart
103–105 Regents Park Road
Primrose Hill
London NW1 8UR
0171 586 9856

**Axor Shower Units –
Brighton**
Hansgrohe Ltd
Units D1/D2
Sandown Park Trading Estate
Royal Mills
Esher
Surrey KT10 8BL
01372 465655
Fax 01372 470670
E-mail sales@hansgrohe.co.uk
Website www.hansgrohe.co.uk

Kitchen units – Brighton
IKEA
The Old Power Station

Valley Park
Purley Way
Croydon CR0 4UZ
0181 208 5601

**Austroflamm stove –
Cornwall**
Stovax Ltd
Falcon Rd
Sowton Industrial Estate
Exeter
Devon EX2 7LF
01392 474000
Fax 01392 219932
E-mail info@stovax.com

Kitchen units – Cornwall
Harvey Jones Ltd
57 New Kings Road
London SW6 4SE
0171 731 3302
Fax 0171 371 0735

**Elica cooker hood –
Cornwall**
D. R. Cooker Hoods Ltd
Elica House
10 Invincible Road
Farnborough
Hampshire GU14 7QU
01252 515355
Fax 01252 540194

Britannia cooker – Cornwall
The Ranger Cooker Co. plc
10–20 Chorley Road
Blackpool FY3 7XQ
01253 300663
Fax 01253 391011
Website: www.rangecooker.co.uk

**Amana fridge freezer –
Cornwall**
NRC Refrigeration Ltd
Vaux Road
Finedon Road Industrial Estate
Wellingborough
Northamptonshire NN8 4TG
01933 388222
Fax 01993 279638

Showers – Cornwall
Mira Showers Ltd
Cromwell Road
Cheltenham GL52 5EP
01242 221221

Interior Fittings

Designer – Doncaster
Roland Leopoldseder
Zeichenburo-Leopoldseder Roland
A-4300 St. Valentin
Rubingerstrasse 14
Austria
00 43 7435 5701948
zbl@magnet.at

Ironmongery – Amersham
Allgood plc
297 Euston Road
London NW1 3AQ
0171 387 9951

Light fittings – Cornwall
Tony Teague (Principal designer)
Design Options Lighting Ltd
3 Eastern Wood Rd.
Langage Business Park
Plympton
Plymouth PL7 5ET
01752 346500
Fax 01752 345536

Wall and floor tiles – Cornwall
Paris Ceramics
583 Kings Road
London SW6 2EH
0171 371 7778
Fax 0171 371 8395
E-mail ceramics@mailhost.atlas.co.uk
Website www.parisceramics.com

Arne Jacobsen door handles – Cornwall
Williams Ironmongery Ltd
Unit 8G1
Halas Industrial Estate
Forge Lane
Halesowen
West Midlands B62 8EB
0121 550 7970
Fax 0121 550 3891

Guttering – Cornwall
Sinclair Cast Iron Water Systems
Sinclair Foundry Products
PO Box 3
Ketley
Telford
Shropshire TF1 4AD
Fax 01952 222794

Airvac extractor fans – Doncaster
Greenwood Air Management
Brookside Industrial Estate
Rustington
West Sussex BN16 3LH
01903 771021
E-mail info@greenwood.btinternet.com

Lights – Newhaven
Micromark (BDC)
550 White Hart Lane
Tottenham
London N17 7RQ
0181 881 2001

Paint – Newhaven
Benetton Paints
Imagica Ltd
Willowbank House
97 Oxford Road
Uxbridge
Middlesex UB8 1LU
01895 819332

Carpets and rugs – Newhaven
Carpetright
The Drove Retail Park
Newhaven
East Sussex BN9 0AU
01273 512094

Lights – Doncaster
Marlin Lighting
Hanworth Trading Estate
Hampton Road West
Feltham
Middlesex TW13 6DR
0181 894 5522
E-mail marketing@marlin.com

Architectural ironmongers – Doncaster
Thew's Ltd
4 Summers Road
Brunswick Business Park
Liverpool L3 4BL
0151 709 9438

Computer Animations

3D diagrams – all builds
Real Time Visualisation
Chiswick House
Chiswick Grove
Morton
Blackpool
Lancashire FY3 9TW
07000 255025
Fax 01253 760767
E-mail realtime@globalnet co.uk
Carpetright

Clothing

Work clothing – Brighton
Snickers Originals Ltd
Unit N3
Gate 4
Meltham Mills Industrial Estate
Knowle Lane
Meltham
Huddersfield HD7 3DS
01484 854488
Fax 01484 854733

Further Information

For information about the Walter Segal method
Mike Dalligan
Walter Segal Trust
Unit 213
16 Baldwin Gardens
London EC1N 7RJ
0171 831 5696

For information about buildings through the ages
Chiltern Open Air Museum
Newland Park
Gorelands Lane
Chalfont St Giles
Buckinghamshire HP8 4AD
01494 872163

For information about straw-bale building courses
Amazon Nails
554 Burnley Road
Todmorden OL14 8JF
01706 814696

For information about straw bales
Francis Henderson
Oathill Farm
Enstone
Chipping Norton
Oxfordshire OX7 4ED
01608 678164

For information about building underground
The Earth Centre
Kilner's Bridge
Doncaster Road
Denaby Main
South Yorkshire DN12 4DY
01709 512000
Fax 01709 512010
E-mail info@earthcentre.org.uk

For information about eco-building and self-build courses
Centre For Alternative Technology
Machynlleth
Powys SY20 9A2
01654 702 400
Website www.cat.org.uk

For information about architects
Royal Institute of British Architects
66 Portland Place
London W1N 4AD
0171 580 5533

Association of Self-Build Architects
The Archway
373 Anlaby Road
Hull HU3 6AB
01482 576319

For information about self-building alternatives
The Permaculture Association
01654 712188

Building Research Establishment
Bucknalls Lane
Garston
Watford
Hertfordshire WD2 7JR
01923 664000
Fax 01923 664010
E-mail enquiries@bre.co.uk
Website www. bre.co.uk

Index

Further Reading

Books

Armor, Murray, *Building Your Own Home*, London: Ebury Press, 1978.
Birchall, Johnston, *The International Co-operative Movement*. Manchester: Manchester University Press, 1997.
Birchall, Johnston, *Co-op, The People's Business*. Manchester: Manchester University Press, 1994.
Blake, Jill, *Healthy Home*. Devon: David & Charles, 1998.
Borer, Pat and Cindy Harris, *Out of the Woods: Ecological Designs for Timber Frame Self Build*. Powys: Walter Segal Trust/CAT, 1994.
Borer, Pat and Cindy Harris, *The Whole House Book: Ecological Building Design and Materials*. Powys: CAT, 1998.
Brinkley, Mark, *The 98/99 Housebuilder's Bible*. Cambridge: Rodelia Ltd, 1997.
Brookes, John, *The New Garden*. London: Dorling Kindersley, 1998.
brroom, Jon and Brian Richardson, *The Self-build Book*. Devon: Green Earth Books, 1995.
Carpenter, Peter (ed.), *'Sod It': An Introduction to Earth Sheltered Development in England and Wales*. Coventry: British Earth Sheltering Association.
Clifton Taylor, Alec, *The Pattern of English Building*. London: Faber & Faber.
Cooke, Robert, *A Simple Guide to Planning Applications*. Romford: Ian Henry Publications, 1987 (2nd edition, 1995).
HM Customs and Excise, *Value Added Tax: VAT Refunds for 'Do It Yourself' Builders and Converters*. London: HM Customs and Excise, 1996.
Howarth, Maggie, *Pebble Mosaics*. Tunbridge Wells: Search Press, 1994.
Kruger, Anne, *H is for Eco-Home*. London: Gaia Books, 1991.
McCloud, Kevin, *The Complete Decorator*. London: Ebury Press, 1996.

McCloud, Kevin, *Lighting Book*. London: Ebury Press, 1995.
Mitchell, Maurice, *The Lemonade Stand: Exploring the Unfamiliar by Building Large-Scale Models*. Powys: CAT.
Pearson, David, *Earth to Spirit*. London: Gaia Books, 1994.
Pearson, David, *The New Natural House Book*. London: Conran Octopus, 1989 (new edition, 1998).
Renshaw, Rosalind, *Design and Build Your Own Home*. London: Built It Magazine, 1995 (new edition, 1997).
Renshaw, Rosalind, *The Build-It Guide to Managing the Build of your own Timber Framed Home*. London: J. M. Dent, 1993.
Speer, Roy and Michael Dade, *How to Find and Buy a Building Plot*. West Sussex: Stonepound Books, 1995 (2nd edition, 1998).
Speer, Roy and Michael Dade, *How to Get Planning Permission*. West Sussex: Stonepound Books, 1998.
Stevenson, Neil, *Annotated Guides: Architecture*. London: Dorling Kindersley, 1997.
Swentzell Steen, Athena, Bill Steen and David Bainbridge with David Eisenberg, *The Straw Bale House*. London: Chelsea Green Publishing.
Talbot, John, *Simply Build Green*. Findhorn: Findhorn Press, 1993 (2nd edition, 1997).
Verner, Yvette, *Creating a Flower Meadow*. Devon: Green Earth Books, 1998.
Woollley, Tom, Sam Kimmins, Paul Harrison and Rob Harrison, *Green Building Handbook*. London: E. & F. N. Spon, 1997.

Magazines

Build It
Homebuilding and Renovating
Selfbuild

Picture Credits

Graeme Strong © Talkback: 2, 6, 10/11, 13, 14, 17, 19, 21, 22, 23, 24, 25, 28, 33, 34, 38, 54, 44, 45, 37, 67, 68, 69, 74, 75, 76(t), 76(b), 78(t), 87, 91, 93, 94/95, 104, 112/113, 113, 116(b), 118, 119, 121, 125, 128, 129, 136/137, 140, 141, 143, 144/145, 148, 151(tl), 151(tr), 151(m), 151(bl), 151(br), 152(t), 152(b), 155, 157(t), 157(b), 158, 161, 163, 165, 169(t), 169(m), 169(b), 170(t), 170(b), 171(b), 172, 174. Edward Schneider © Channel 4 Books: 56, 58(l), 58(r), 59, 60, 73, 78(b), 89, 109, 123, 117, 133, 139, 166, 171(t), 171(m), 173, 176, 177. Kevin McCloud: 159. © Barbara Jones/Amazon Nails: 83(t), 83(b). © Martine Hamilton Knight/Arcaid: 7(t). © Ken Kirkwood/Arcaid: 8. © Richard Bryant/Arcaid: 63, 98(t), 98(b), 99(t), 99(b). © Scott Frances/Arcaid: 63. British Earth Sheltering Association (David Woods): 79, 80. Centre for Alternative Technology: 82, 154. Elizabeth Whiting & Associates (Mark Luscombe-Whyte): 62. Future Systems (Richard Davies): 88. The Lime Centre (Bob Bennett): 86(t), 86(b). Realtime: 49. © Duncan Maxwell/Robert Harding Picture Library: 7(b). © Robert Francis/Robert Harding Picture Library 26(t).

© James Merrell/Robert Harding Picture Library: 57. Andrew Tate: 30, 55, 103, 156. Carpenter Oak & Woodland Co. Ltd: 9, 26(b), 65, 175. Colin Harwood: 48. David Sheppard: 40, 46(b), 51. Neil Winder: 39, 47, 52. Jeremy Till and Sarah Wigglesworth: 35, 84, 100/101, 149. David Grandorge courtesy of Jeremy Till and Sarah Wigglesworth: 46(t). Rob Roy: 116(t), 134. Tim Cox and Julia Brock: 44.

Acknowledgements

Thanks to Janet Payne of Payne Baker Rees Architects for painstakingly reading the manuscript and acting as a consultant on this book. TalkBack Productions is grateful for the co-operation of all the suppliers and wishes to acknowledge the assistance of the following decorating, furnishing and technical suppliers: Cargo Home Stores, Chelsom Lighting, Christopher Wray Lighting, David Wainwright, Garden Style, Habitat, Kodak, The Pier, Pots and Pithoi and PUS Wrought Iron Furniture. Thanks also to Emma Tait at Channel 4 Books and Laurence Bradbury at Bradbury & Williams.